THE PALLAVAS

BY

G. JOUVEAU-DUBREUIL
Doctor of the University of Paris,
Professor, College, Pondicherry.

TRANSLATED FROM FRENCH

BY

V. S. SWAMINADHA DIKSHITAR, B.A., L.T.,
Officier d'Acadimic
Professor of English, Colonial College, Pondicherry

GYAN

Published by

GYAN

Gyan Publishing House
5, Ansari Road
Daryaganj, New Delhi-110002
Phone: 011-47034999, 9811692060
E-mail: books@gyanbooks.com

Distribution Network
gyanbooks.com
India, USA, Canada, UK, Australia, France

ISBN : 978-81-212-3869-4 (PB)
First Published, 1917

2nd Impression 2020

Printed at: Gyan Press, Delhi.

The Pallavas
Author: G. Jouveau-Dubreuil

THE PALLAVAS

THE

PALLAVAS

BY

G. JOUVEAU-DUBREUIL

Doctor of the University of Paris,
Professor, College, Pondicherry.

TRANSLATED FROM FRENCH

BY

V. S. SWAMINADHA DIKSHITAR, B.A., L.T.,

Officier d'Académie
Professor of English, Colonial College, Pondicherry.

PONDICHERRY:
SOLD BY THE AUTHOR,
6, DUMAS STREET.

1917

WORKS BY THE SAME AUTHOR.

IN FRENCH:

Archéologie du Sud de l'Inde—[Annales du Musée Guimet-Bibliothèque d'Etudes—Tomes vingt-sixième et vingt-septième.]

TOME I.—*Architecture*— Avec 71 figures et 64 planches hors texte—192 pages. Librairie Paul Geuthner, 13, rue Jacob, Paris, 1914.

TOME II.—*Iconographie*— Avec 40 figures et 44 planches hors texte—146 pages. Librairie Paul Geuthner, 13, rue Jacob, Paris, 1914.

IN ENGLISH:

Pallava Antiquities, Vol. I.— With 32 plates.—Probsthain and Co., 41, Great Russell Street, London, 1916.

Dravidian Architecture: with 35 figures.—Edited with Preface and Notes by S. Krishṇaswāmi Aiyangar, M.A., M.R.A.S., F.R. Hist. S., Professor of Indian History and Archæology, University of Madras. Printed at the S. P. C. K. Press, Vepery, Madras, 1917.

IN PREPARATION:

Pallava Antiquities, Vol. II.

CHAPTER I.

THE ROMAN ORIGIN OF PALLAVA ART.

I do not know if any author has so far attempted to ascertain what kind of art flourished at the time of the first kings of the Pallava dynasty. That is what we shall try to determine in this chapter.

There is a document which is particularly important for a study of the early history of the Pallavas; it is the Viripara plates discovered at Mayidavôlu, a village situated at a distance of 12 miles from Narasarâopet in the Guntûr district which lies on the southern bank of the Kṛishṇâ.

From his capital, Kâñchîpura, and in the 10th year of the reign of his father whose name is not given, the heir-apparent (Yuva-Mahârâja) Śivaskandavarman, of the Pallava dynasty and of Bhâradvâja Gôtra, sent to the governors of Dhaññakaḍa an order concerning the village of Viripara, situated in the province of Ândhrâpatha (*Ep. Ind.*, Vol. VI, p. 84.)

There is no doubt that this prince belongs to the dynasty whose history we are studying, for it is expressly stated that Śivaskandavarman lived at Kâñchî, and was of the family of the Pallavas and of Bhâradvâja Gôtra.

Again, as the plates were discovered in the Guntûr District and the village for which they were engraved was in Ândhrâpatha, and as the order was issued to the officers of Dhaññakaḍa, that is to say, the town of Amarâvatî, it is certain that the Pallava princes of this period reigned not only over Toṇḍai maṇḍalam, that is to say, the province of Kâñchî, but also over the country up to the banks of the Kṛishṇâ which was occupied by the Ândhras and in which was situated the town of Amarâvatî where, in the middle of the 2nd century, King Puḷumâyi II. built the white marble Stûpa, the sculptures of which, almost entirely Roman in workmanship, now adorn the Madras Museum.

The Pallavas have thus succeeded the Ândhras on the banks of the Kṛishṇâ; but how long after and at what epoch?

We shall now show, that, in all probability, the father of Śivaskandavarman of the Pallava dynasty reigned at Amarâvatî shortly after Puḷumâyi II. had built the famous Stûpa.

The gift of the village of Viripara bears only the date of the year of the king's reign; however, the alphabet in which it is written would enable us to determine the date, if we have any points of comparison.

Fortunately, in this case, we have such points of comparison: The Mayidavôlu plates are written in the same alphabet as the plates found at Koṇḍamûdi (a village situated in the Tenâli Tâluk, Guntûr District). And in its language and its phraseology the Koṇḍamûdi document resembles so much the Kârlê inscription of Gautamiputra Śâtakarṇi, and the Nâsik inscription of Vâśishthîputra Puḷumâyi, that there cannot be any great difference of date between them:

« The alphabet of this inscription shows that he must have » lived in the same period as the Pallava prince Śivaskandavarman » who issued the Mayidavôlu plates. Further, the language and » phraseology of the inscription are so similar to the Nâsik » inscriptions [a still closer resemblance exists between Jaya- » varman's plates and the Kârlê inscription No. 19 (*A. S. W. I.* » Vol. IV, p. 112)] of Gautamîputra Śâtakarṇi (Nos. 4 and 5) » [Dr. Bhagwanlal Indraji's in *Bombay Gazetteer* Vol. XVI, and » Inscriptions from the cave temples of Western India—*Kârlê*] of » Vâsishthîputra Puḷumâyi (No. 3), that Jayavarman's date cannot » have been very distant from that of those two Ândhra Kings.» (*Ep. Ind.* Vol. VI, No. 31, p. 315).

If we bear in mind that it was Vâśisthîputra Puḷumâyi who built the Stûpa at Amarâvati, we may conclude that the Pallava king, father of Śivaskandavarman, who engraved the Mayidavôlu plates, reigned at Amarâvatî shortly after Puḷumâyi II.

A strange coincidence indeed: the son of this Puḷumâyi reigned from 177 to 184 A.D., under the name of Śivaskanda which was also the name of the son of the Pallava king.

Is this coincidence something purely accidental? We may believe it is not. In fact it is possible that the Pallava king had married the daughter of Śivaskanda Śâtakarṇi and that the "Yuvamahârâja" of the Pallava dynasty received, according to the custom of the Hindus, the name of the Ândhra king who was his grandfather.

Since we are now dealing with suppositions, we shall say a few words here about the theory of the Persian origin of the Pallavas.

The father of Puḷumâyi II. had fought with the Pahlavas, and this same Puḷumâyi had to struggle against the satrap Rudradāman, who, about the year 150 A.D. had for minister a Pahlava called Suviśâkha. (*Ind. Ant.*, VII, 257—Junagadh Insc.) Relying upon the analogy of names, certain authors think that these Pahlavas, who fought with the Andhras, succeeded in establishing a kingdom for themselves between the Kṛishṇâ and the Pâlar and founded the Pallava dynasty.

This theory is subject to variations in its details. For example, we may suppose that the Pahlavas took possession of one part of the Ândhra empire not by conquest but by marriages such as the one that is supposed to have taken place between the father of Śivaskandavarman and the daughter of the Ândhra King of the same name.

Similar marriages between the Ândhras and those of other dynasties have surely taken place; we know that Puḷumâyi II. married the daughter of the satrap Rudradâman, whose minister was a Pahlava.

All these hypotheses are based on the similarity of names: Yuvamahârâja Śivaskandavarman and Śivaskanda Śâtakarṇi, Pahlavas and Pallavas; but they are contestable.

All that we can consider as certaian is that the Pallava King who reigned at Amarâvatí when the Mayidavôlu plates were engraved lived shortly after Puḷumâyi II. who built the Stûpa at Amarâvatî; but it is not possible to say exactly how long after.

The Ândhra dynasty came to an end about 236 A.D. There is nothing, however, to prove that the Pallavas did not succeed the Ândhras many years earlier at Amarâvatî, and that the prince Śivaskandavarman was not the contemporary of the last Ândhra kings whose kingdom had now become much smaller. In that case, the Mayidavôlu plates may be dated about 200 A.D. If, however, the Pallavas succeeded the Ândhras after 236 A.D. it must have been immediately after, for the resemblance between the Mayidavôlu plates and Jayavarman's plates discovered at Koṇḍamûdi is so close that we cannot suppose that more than a century would have elapsed between Śivaskandavarman and Puḷumâyi II.

We can therefore conclude that the Pallava kings reigned at Amarâvatî in the first half of the third century after Christ, that is, about 50 years after the famous Stûpa was built. These kings reigned over a very extensive territory: their empire extended from the banks of the Pâlâr to those of the Kṛishṇâ. They were therefore powerful and glorious.

What about the art in this kingdom? There is no doubt about the answer. Pallava art at the time of Śivaskandavarman cannot be very different from that which flourished at the time when Puḷumâyi II built the Stûpa at Amarâvatî.

A visit to the remains that are kept in the Madras Museum is enough to convince one that this art had attained great perfection.

The subjects are Buddhistic, the costumes and the ornaments are Hindu, but their workmanship is European.

But, above all, it is in the representation of the human body that the European influence manifests itself. The hair is curled in the Greek manner, the face is symmetrical, the limbs are sculptured according to the rules of Anatomy with conspicuous muscles, and some of them are dressed in clothes that remind us of the Roman toga.

This Indo-European art was not peculiar only to the banks of the Kṛishṇâ; it was found throughout India and specially in Gandhâra.

At this epoch, the Roman Empire extended its influence over almost the whole of the civilised world and was also connected with India in various ways.

How long did this influence last? There is no doubt that it disappeared from South India in the VII century, whereas it was probably not introduced there before the Christan era. It attained its zenith probably in the II and the III centuries. There is no doubt that in its origin the Pallava art was strongly influenced by the principles of the Latin Art.

In many places on the banks of the Kṛishṇâ, we find sculptured marbles of which the subjects are Buddhistic and the workmanship Roman. These are the bas-reliefs that once adorned the Stûpas or the mutilated images of Buddha. Up to the present they have always been attributed to the Ândhras. This view, I am sure, is not always correct.

The Graeco-Buddhistic art did not certainly disappear with the Ândhra dynasty. It is not likely that the technical methods

Plate I

Roman head of Buddha

(Discovered by the Author near Bezwada.)

had discovered at Bezwada. The other head and the trunk have since been brought over by the Government to the Madras Museum.

Was this Indo-Roman art confined to the banks of the Kṛishṇa, or did it extend through the whole Pallava empire? The latter is very probable; the Buddhists at Kâñchîpuram built, in their capital, Stûpas that were perhaps in the same style as those in the north of the Empire. The only researches, so far attempted, into the Buddhistic remains at Kâñchî have been made by M. R. Ry. T. A. Gopinatha Rao when on a short visit to the town, and his rapid investigation has been very fruitful in as much as he has discovered, in the last prâkâra of the Kâmâkshî-dêvî temple, a Roman statue of Buddha which is shown in Fig. I of the article "Bauddha vestiges in Kâñchîpura" by T. A. Gopinatha Rao (*Ind. Ant.*, Vol. XLIV, Part DLVII, June 1915). If we compare the head of this statue with that of the one I have found at Bezwada, and the trunk with the one since brought over to the Madras Museum, we shall find that the resemblance between them is complete.

We can therefore conclude by saying, that, at Kâñchîpuram as well as at Amarâvatî and Bezwada, the Pallava Art, inspired by Roman models, attained great perfection at the time of those early Pallava kings.

CHAPTER II.

THE VÂYALÛR INSCRIPTION.

The record found at Mayidavôlu is written in Prâkṛit. There are also two others of the same kind; but the other Pallava records are in Sanskrit; the former are surely the oldest and can be considered to belong to the III century.

One of these two records (*Ep. Ind.* Vol. I, p. 2), that of Hîrahaḍagalli, is dated in the 8th year of the reign of Sivaskandavarman, King of Kâñchî, who is of the Pallava dynasty and Bhâradvâja gôtra and who by this document confirms a gift made by his father Bappa-dēva. We may suppose that this Śivaskanda was the person who was "Yuvamahârâja" when the Mayidavôlu gift was made, but we are not quite sure of it.

This record is specially important as it shows the extent of the Pallava empire. These plates (discovered in the Bellary District) mention the province of Sâtâhani (Sâtâhani-rattha) as forming part of the Pallava kingdom. This province comprised a portion of the Bellary District. Thus, we know that the Pallavas reigned over an empire, which, having Kâñçhîpuram for its capital, extended not only along the Coromandel coast up to the mouth of the Kṛishṇâ, but also to the West, in the Deccan, up to the banks of the Tungabhadra river.

Here also the Pallavas had succeeded the Ândhras. The inscription discovered at Myâkadoni, in the Bellary district, (*G.O.* No. 99, 29th August 1916.—Report on Epigraphy for 1915-1916) says that King Puḷumâyi II. reigned about 140 A.D. over the province of Sâtâvahani-hâra which is none other than Sâtâhani-rattha of the Hîrahaḍagalli copper-plates.

We see then that, at first, the Pallava empire extended more in the Deccan than in the Tamil country; there is nothing to prove that it comprised the banks of the Kâvêrî; the Trichinopoly region was probably occupied by the Chôḷas; on the contrary, we are sure that the Pallavas reigned over the country extending from Bellary to Bezwada, that is to say, over an important portion of the Ândhra empire. These geographical considerations lead to the probability of the theory that the Pallavas were a Northern dynasty, who, having contracted marriages with the princesses of the Ândhra dynasty, inherited a portion of the Southern part of the Ândhra empire.

The other record was discovered in the District of Guṇtûr (*Ep. Ind.*, Vol. VIII, p. 143). In the reign of Vijayaskandavarman, Chârudêvi, wife of "Yuvamahârâja" Vijaya-Buddhavarman, a Pallava prince of the Bhâradvâja gôtra, and mother of Buddhyaṅkura, made a gift to the temple of Nârâyana at Dâlûra.

The alphabet of these plates resembles that of the Hîrahaḍagalli plates. However, as the name of the king is not exactly the same, we cannot, with certainty, identify Vijayaskanda with Śivaskanda.

We shall conclude by saying that the three Prâkṛit records (those of Mayidavôlu and Hîrahaḍagalli, and the grant made by Chârudêvi) found in the districts of Guntûr and Bellary, prove that many princes of the Pallava dynasty of Kâñchîpuram—(1) the father of Yuvamahârâja Śivaskandavarman [called Bappadêva in the Hîrahadagalli plates], (2) Yuvamahârâja Śivaskandavarman, (3) Mahârâja Śivaskandavarman, (4) Mahârâja Vijayaskandavarman, (5) Yuvamahârâja Vijaya Buddhavarman, (6) His son Buddhyaṅkura (2 and 3 being perhaps one and the same person)—reigned towards the III century, not only over Toṇḍai Maṇḍalam, but also over the lands bordering the Kṛishṇâ and Tungabhadra, and so over a great part of the Telugu country.

We know from the inscription on the pillar at Allâhâbâd that about 340 A.D. the great emperor Samudragupta vanquished Vishṇugôpa, King of Kâñchî.

Certain authors have supposed: (*a*) that Vishṇugôpa was a Pallava; (*b*) that Samudragupta advanced as far as Kâñchî (Conjeeveram) in the Tamil country.

I think that the last conclusion is not correct. I believe that Samudragupta never entered the Tamil country but that Vishṇugôpa was, in fact, a Pallava king. We know that the kings of Kâñchî reigned on the banks of the Kṛishṇâ; it is, therefore, very likely that events happened as mentioned below: Samudragupta came from the North of India and vanquished the kings who reigned at Pithâpuram, Mahêndragiri, and Kothûra. When they saw him advance to the South of the Gôdâvarî, Mantarâja who reigned near the Colair lake, his neighbour, the King of Vengî, Vishṇugôpa, King of Kâñchî who reigned on the right bank of the Kṛishṇâ and his neighbour Ugrasêna, King of Pâlakka, formed a coalition to stop the invader. But he affirms that he was the victor; and until the contrary is proved we have to believe in his words.

Be that as it may, it is probable that Samudragupta did not care to advance more to the South in a country which must have been difficult of access, and so returned to the North.

Let us now examine the Sanskṛit records.

Five copper plates:

1° Ôṁgôdu No. 1 (*G.O.* No. 99, 29 Aug. 1616, Part II, No. 3),
2° Uruvupalli (*Ind. Ant.* Vol. V, p. 50),
3° Ôṁgôdu No. 2 (*G.O.* No. 99, 29 Aug. 1916, Part II, No. 4),
4° Pikira (*Ep. Ind.*, Vol. VIII, p. 159),
5° Mâṅgaḷûr (*Ind. Ant.*, Vol. V, p. 154),

enable us to establish with certainty the following genealogy:

Kumâravishṇu
|
Skandavarman (I)
|
Vîravarman
|
Skandavarman (II)
|
Yuvamahârâja Vishṇugôpa
|
Siṁhavarman.

These six princes belonged to the Pallava dynasty and Bhâradvâja gôtra. There is nothing, however, to prove that their capital was Kâñchîpuram. It is also probable that, had Kâñchî been their capital, they would have dated their grants from there. But Skandavarman II. was encamped at Tâṁbrâpa when he made the Ôṁgôḍu No. 1 grant; Yuvamahârâja Vishṇugôpa was at Palakkada when he made the Uruvupalli grant; Siṁhavarman was at Daśanapuram when he made the Mâṅgaḷûr grant and at Menmatura at the time of the Pikira grant. It is therefore probable that these three sovereigns never reigned at Kâñchîpuram. The geographical position of these towns from which the several grants have been made is not known; but we know accurately a region which formed one of the provinces of their kingdom. The two Ôṁgôḍu records mention "Karmmâ-râshtra" as forming part of their empire, and this district is often mentioned in the grants made by the Eastern Châlukyas. We know also that the village of Chendalûr (*Ep. Ind.*, Vol. VIII, p. 233) which is only another name for Chandalûru, a village in the Ongole taluq of the Guntûr district, was situated in this province. Besides, it is also probable that the village of Ôṁgôḍu was adjacent to Santarâvûru where the plates were discovered. Santarâvûru is in the Bâpatla taluq of the Guntûr district.

There is therefore no doubt that the environs of the present town of Ongole watered by the river Gundlakamma was named Karmmâ-râshtra at the time of the ancient Pallavas. There is no other information about these kings except their genealogy.

The word "Yuvamahârâja" preceding the name of Vishṇugôpa shows that he never reigned. He has however made a grant to the village of Uruvupalli in the 11th year of the reign of Siṁhavarman. So, Vishṇugôpa was probably the brother of a king named Siṁhavarman.

The grant of the village of Chûra (*G. O.* No. 920, 4th Aug. 1914, Part II, No. 1) enables us to suppose that the donor Vijaya-Vishṇugôpavarman was the son of Siṁhavarman and grandson of Yuvamahârâja Vishṇugôpa, though he is called in the Chûra plates "Maharâja" and not "Yuvamahârâja".

An isolated copper plate relating to a grant made at Daśanapuram by the great-grandson of King Śrî-Vîra-Kôrchavarman, has been discovered at Darśi (Nellûr District) [*Ep. Ind.*, Vol. I, p. 397]. Be that as it may, we must bear in mind the incontestable fact that a dynasty of six or seven Pallava kings reigned over the Telugu country about the V century of the Christian era.

But what connection had they with the kings of Kâñchîpuram? we do not know it exactly.

We may suppose that the Chôḷas occupied Kâñchî for the time being and about the V century drove back the Pallavas to the north of the kingdom.

The existence of a dynasty of Chôḷa princes in the Telugu country seems to confirm this presumption (*G. O.* No. 518, 18th July 1905, Part II, No. 5).

It is again not improbable that the Pallavas divided themselves into two dynasties, one reigning in the Tamil and the other in the Telugu country.

We know very little about the ancient kings of Kâñchî.

At Chendalûr in the Ongole taluq of the Guntûr district there has been found the record of a grant relating to this same village of Chendalûra in the "Karmâ-râshtra", which contains the following genealogy:

Skandavarman.
|
Kumâravishṇu (I).
|
Buddhavarman.
|
Kumâravishṇu (II).

The last of these was a Pallava king of Kâñchî. As we see from the geographical position of Chandalûr, this king reigned not only at Kâñchî, but also in the Telugu country and over this very "Karmâ-râshtra" which belonged to the Telugu line of kings about whom we have spoken just now.

One is tempted to identify Kumâravishṇu II with the first king of the Telugu dynasty: but the alphabet of the Chendalûr plates, instead of being more archaic, appears to be more developed than that of the Oṁgôḍu, Uruvupalli, Pikîra, Mâñgaḷûr copper-plates. I shall however propound a theory concerning the Chendalûr plates. The alphabet of this record is very peculiar and does not resemble that of any other documents of this kind; I am therefore led to believe that the Chendalûr plates are a copy of an older one. In that case it would be possible to identify one of the two Kumâravishṇus of the Chendalûr plates with Kumâravishṇu of the Ômgôḍu No. 1 plates.

The Udayêndiram copper-plates (*Ep. Ind.*, Vol. III, p. 142) give the line:

Skandavarman
|
Siṁhavarman
|
Skandavarman
|
Nandivarman,

the last being a king of Kâñchî. Unfortunately, this record is written in characters which are not very ancient; there is no means of knowing if it is a forgery or a copy of a genuine document.

The Jain work called "Lokavibhâga," discovered by M.R.Ry. R. Narasiṁhachar, is dated Ś. 380 (458 A. D.), the 22nd year of the reign of the Pallava king Siṁhavarman; this evidence is rather suspicious, and besides it does not say which Siṁhavarman it was and to what branch of the Pallava family he belonged.

The Penugoṇḍa plates (*G.O.* No. 920, 4th Aug. 1914. Part II., No. 4 and J. R. A. S. Oct. 1915) mention two Pallava kings Siṁhavarman and Skandavarman, but the age of these plates is not known.

The Pallavas themselves have attempted to answer the important question who were the ancestors of the Pallavas of the Siṁhavishṇu dynasty. The Kaśakûḍi plates give a few of the names of kings (*S.I.I.*, Vol. II, Part III. p. 356).

The Vêlûrpaḷaiyam plates (*S.I.I.*, Vol. II, Part V, p. 510) give us more information; but, unfortunately, they do not give us a complete list. On the contrary, this author warns us that the kings he mentions, are only a few among the numerous predecessors of Siṁhavishṇu. These isolated names do not enable us to build up a genealogy.

Moreover this record which is dated in the IX century, not being relatively ancient, we do not know how far we can rely on it.

The Vâyalûr inscription presents much greater guarantee as it is the most ancient genealogy of this kind. Whereas the Kaśakûḍi and Vêlûrpaḷaiyam plates are dated during the time of the princes of the dynasty of Nandivarman, the Vayâlûr inscription is of the time of a prince of the dynasty of Siṁhavishṇu.

Besides, this inscription gives the names of such a large number of kings that it seems to be a complete list of them in the order of their succession.

It is for these two reasons that the Vâyalûr inscription becomes extremely interesting.

The Vâyalûr inscription (No. 368 of 1908) is very much damaged: The report on Epigraphy for 1908-09 (*G.O.* No. 536, 28th July 1909—Part II, No. 17, p. 77) speaks of it only in a very summary manner. The order of succession of the predecessors of Siṁha'ishṇu is not given in the report, but it is precisely this order that it would be interesting to know.

The report says:

« The pillar in the Vyâghrapurîśvara temple is a very
» interesting one on account of the genealogical record which
» is engraved on it. The latter begins with the usual mythical
» names Brahma, Aṅgiras, Bṛihaspati, Śaṁyu, Bhâradvâja, Drôṇa,
» Aśvatthâman, and Pallava. Then, the quasi-historical names
» Aśôka, Harigupta, Âryavarman and others are mentioned.
» After these, the names of nearly twenty-five kings are registered
» whose relations to one another are not specified. The order in
» which the known names are mentioned at the end suggests,
» however, that these twenty-five are also to be taken in the order
» of descent. Among these occur the following which are already
» familiar to us from copper-plate inscriptions:—(1) Mahêndra-
» varman (once), (2) Karanda (Kalindavarman ?) (once), (3) Vishṇu-
» gôpa (thrice), (4) Kumâravishṇu (twice), (5) Buddhavarman
» (twice), (6) Skandavarman (five times), (7) Siṁhavarman (four
» times), (8) Vîravarman (once), and (9) Nandivarman (once). In
» many places the record is damaged and the names are not
» legible. If, however, the whole of the inscription is made out, it
» will perhaps establish a connection more definite than that
» hitherto set forth by the copper-plates between the Pallavas of
» the Prâkṛit records, those of the Sanskṛit records, and those of
» the Siṁhavishṇu line. The Amarâvatî pillar epigraph (which is
» evidently a copy of some older record) gives a list of early
» Pallava Kings some of whom also occur in the Vâyalûr inscrip-
» tion. After mentioning the twenty-five names above referred to,
» the latter introduces Siṁhavishṇu for the first time. From him
» were descended apparently in the order of father and son,
» Mahêndravarman I, Narasiṁhavarman I, Mahêndravarman II,
» and Paramêśvaravarman I. His son was Râjasiṁha 'the (very)
» king of lions on the high mountain (viz.) the prosperous Pallava
» family'...................................... ».

Seeing the importance of the Vâyalûr inscription for a history of the Pallavas, I went over there with the object of studying it myself on the spot.

It is engraved on a cubical pillar of the Pallava style and runs round it in the form of a helix. It begins with the well-known series of names: Brahma, Aṅgiras, Bṛihaspati, Śaṁyu, Bharadvâja, Drôṇa, Aśvathâman, Pallava, Aśôka, Harigupta

Âryavarman, and then two or three names hardly legible, and then Kâḷinda, Byâmalla, [E]kamalla.

After this last name begins a series of 36 names. The estampage of this part of the inscription is given in *Plate II.*

1. Vimala
2. Koṅkaṇika
3. Kâḷabhartṛi
4. Chûtapallava
5. Vîrakûrcha
6. Chandravarman
7. Karâḷa
8. Vishṇugôpa
9. Skandamûla
10. Kâṇagôpa
11. Vîrakûrcha
12. Skandavarman
13. Kumâravishṇu
14. Buddhavarman
15. Skandavarman
16. Kumâravishṇu
17. Buddhavarman
18. Skandavarman
19. Vishṇugôpa
20. Vishṇudâsa
21. Skandavarman
22. Siṁhavarman
23. Vîravarman
24. Skandavarman
25. Siṁhavarman
26. Skandavarman
27. Nandivarman (I)
28. Siṁhavarman
29. Siṁhavarman
30. Visṇugôpa
31. Siṁhavarman
32. Siṁhavishṇu
33. Mahêndravarman (I)
34. Narasiṁhavarman (I)
35. Mahêndravarman (II)
36. Paramêsvaravarman (I).

A fact of very great importance is that in the legendary series of ancestors of the kings belonging to the dynasty of

Plate II.

The Vayalūr inscription.

Siṁhavishṇu there are personages called Âryavarman and Koṅkaṇika, names that are surely of Western Gaṅga origin.

The Penugoṇḍa plates (*G. O.* No. 920, 4th Aug. 1914, Part II, No. 4, p. 83) which are the only authentic records that we have about the ancient W. Gaṅgas give the dynasty:

Koṅkaṇivarman
|
Mâdhava
|
Âryavarman
|
Siṁhavarman.

The presence of names of Gaṅga origin in the legendary portion of the list of Pallavas goes to confirm the fact that those kings had political relations with the Pallavas as is shown by the Penugoṇḍa plates: (Âryavarman and Siṁhavarman were crowned by Pallava kings).

Let us now compare the Vâyalûr inscription with the Kaśâkûḍi plates.

The series of names is the same up to Pallava.

Between Pallava and Siṁhavishṇu the list of names given in the Kaśâkûḍi plates is rather short. However, as at Vâyalûr, we read: Aśôka, Kâṇagôpa, Skandavarman, Vishṇugôpa, Vîrakûrcha, Simhavarman. Kalindavarman of Kaśâkûḍi is probably none other than Kâḷinda of Vâyalûr.

If we compare the Vâyalûr inscription with that of Amarâvati (*S. I. I.*, Vol. I, p. 25) which, we know, is not an ancient one, we find little resemblance between them.

On the contrary, the Vâyalûr inscription exactly coincides with that of Vêlûrpâḷaiyam. The Vâyalûr list is complete; but in the Vâyalûr plates, we have many "et cætera" in place of names.

After a few names which are all of them found in the Vâyalûr list—Aśôka, Kâḷabhartṛi, Chûtapallava,—the coincidence becomes complete:

Vêlûrpâḷaiyam.	*Vâyalûr.*
Vîrakûrcha	(11) Vîrakûrcha
|	
Skandaśishya	(12) Skandavarman
|	
Kumâravishṇu	(13) Kumâravishṇu
|	
Buddhavarman	(14) Buddhavarman

The Vêlûrpâḷaiyam plates say that (11) Vîrakûrcha was the first who "grasped the complete insignia of royalty", that is to say, that his predecessors were not kings and that Vîrakûrcha was the first Pallava king.

In fact, with these four kings we enter into the domain of history leaving the series of legendary names behind.

The existence of a king called Vîrakûrcha is proved by the plate discovered at Darśi (*Ep. Ind.*, Vol. I, p. 397). The existence of a king of the name of Skandaśishya is established by the Tirukkaḻukkunṟam inscription. [*Ep. Ind.*, Vol. III, p. 277].

This king is identified by the Vâyalûr inscription with (No. 12) Skandavarman. This identification admits of no doubt since in both the inscriptions he is mentioned as the son of Vîrakûrcha, and father of Kumâravishṇu and grand-father of Buddhavarman.

It is to be noted that the name Skandavarman given in the Vâyalûr inscription to the second Pallava king (Vîrakûrcha being the first) is also the most ancient name known to history. In fact, the donor of the Mayidavôlu plates is called "Yuvamahârâja" Śivaskandavarman; the donor of the Hîrahaḍagalli plates goes under the name of Śiva-Skandavarman; and the names Skandavarman and Buddhavarman figure in the grant of Chârudêvi that has been found in the Guntûr district (*Ep. Ind.*, Vol. VIII, p. 143).

The list :

Skandavarman
|
Kumâravishṇu
|
Buddhavarman

is the same as the one found in the genealogy given in the Chendalûr plates (*Ep. Ind.*, Vol. VIII, No. 23, p. 233) which we have supposed to be a copy of an ancient record; so we have to note that the Vêlûrpâḷaiyam and the Vâyalûr records place them among the earliest kings.

Let us now conclude by saying that with (11) Vîrakûrcha we deal no more with the legendary series of descendants of Pallava but with the historic line of kings.

What makes the coincidence existing between the Vâyalûr and Vêlûrpâḷaiyam records interesting is that the latter gives an important information :

« (V. 6)... *Vîrakûrcha*, of celebrated name, who simultaneously with (the hand of) the daughter of the chief of serpents » grasped also the complete insignia of royalty and became » famous.»

We have already concluded from this passage that Vîrakûrcha was the first Pallava king.

Here we have to make a remark : the Vêlûrpâḷaiyam plates together with the Vâyalûr inscription lead us to think that, in the Pallava family, there existed the following tradition which was probably perpetuated from century to century. "The earliest Pallavas were not kings, and they were alien to South India. One of them married the daughter of one of the kings of that country and thus became a king himself. Skandavarman was a son born of this marriage."

Is it not strange that this tradition coincides exactly with the theory that we have propounded in the preceding Chapter ?

A Pahlava married the daughter of the Ândhra King Śiva-Skanda and thus became the first king of the Pallava dynasty. The son born of this union was Śiva-Skandavarman.

We should not rely too much on the order of succession of the kings given in the Vâyalûr inscription after (11) Vîrakûrcha. It has to be noted, however, that among the early kings we find (19) Vishṇugôpa who must be identified with Vishṇugôpa of Kâñchî who was the adversary of Samudragupta about the year 339 A.D.

But, from which king does the order of succession given in the Vâyalûr inscription become trustworthy ? I believe it is from (23) Vîravarman. In fact, if we compare the Vâyalûr series with the genealogies given in the undermentioned plates :

Ôṁgôdu No. 1 [O., 1]
Uruvupalli [Ur.]
Ôṁgôdu No. 2 [O., 2]
Pikîra [P.]
Mâṅgaḷûr [M.]
Chûra [C.]
Udayendiram [Ud.]

we obtain the following table in which the numbers indicate those of the Vâyalûr list:

		Approximative dates: A. D.
(23) Vîravarman [O., 1] [Ur.] [O., 2] [P.] [M.]		422
(24) Skandavarman [O., 1] [Ud.] [Ur.] [O., 2] [P.] [M.] [C.]		450
(25) Siṁhavarman [Ud.] [Ur.]	Yuvamahârâja Vishṇugôpa [Ur.] [O., 2] [P.] [M.] [C.]	478
(26) Skandavarman [Ud.]	(29) Siṁhavarman [O., 2] [P.] [M.] [C.]	506
(27) Nandivarman [Ud.]	(30) Vishṇugôpa [C.]	534
(28) Siṁhavarman	(31) Siṁhavarman	562
	(32) Siṁhavishṇu	590

I think that the Vâyalûr record is extremely important on account of the series:

(24) Skandavarman
(25) Siṁhavarman
(26) Skandavarman
(27) Nandivarman

which exactly coincides with the genealogy given in the Udayendiram plates (*Ep. Ind.*, Vol. III, p. 142). We have already said, that, the alphabet of these plates not being ancient, we cannot say how far they can be trusted. The deciphering of the Vâyalûr inscription has shown that this genealogy is quite right and that the Udayendiram plates are a true copy of an earlier record.

The succession list:

(29) Siṁhavarman
(30) Vishṇugôpa
(31) Siṁhavarman
(32) Siṁhavishṇu

unites the dynasty of Siṁhavishṇu with that of Vishṇugôpa of the Chûra plates, (*G. O.* No. 920, 4th Aug. 1914, Part. II., No. 1).

The Uruvupalli plates prove that (25) Siṁhavarman was the brother of Yuvamahârâja Vishṇugôpa and that both of them were the sons of (24) Skandavarman and grandsons of (23) Vîravarman.

It is probable that (24) Skandavarman did not reign at Kâñchî, since the Ôṁgôdu No. 1 plates are dated from Tâṁbrâpa camp.

It is also probable that his son (25) Siṁhavarman resumed possession of Kâñchî and confided to his brother Yuvamahârâja Vishṇugôpa the government of the Northern provinces (Guntûr and Nellore Districts) in which were situated Palakkada, Daśanapura and Mênmâtura as well as the districts of Veṅgorâshtra, Muṇḍarâshtra and Karmarâshṭra. Vishṇugôpa was never crowned and always remained a subordinate of his brother; that is why he is called Yuvamahârâja.

His son (29) Siṁhavarman became independent.

So there were two dynasties simultaneously: in fact, when (30) Vishṇugôpa reigned at Palakkada (Chûra plates), (27) Nandivarman reigned at Kâñchî.

It is probable that (31) Siṁhavarman or (32) Siṁhavishṇu took possession of Kâñchî.

Siṁhavishṇu is then a descendant of the dynasty that reigned at Palakkada. That is why the Vâyalûr inscription gives first the names of the kings of the dynasty of (27) Nandivarman of Kâñchî, and then of those of the dynasty of Palakkada.

Yuvamahârâja Vishṇugôpa is not mentioned in the Vâyalûr list as he was never crowned king.

In the preceding table, we have given in the margin the approximate dates of the predecessors of Siṁhavishṇu. Starting from Siṁhavishṇu who lived at the end of the VI century, about 590 A.D., we have given to each generation an average duration of 28 years.

This calculation seems to be correct, for we find, that, according to it, (25) Siṁhavarman must have lived in 470 A.D. And if we can depend on what is said in the "Lokavibhâga" discovered by M. R. Ry. R. Narasiṃhachar, there seems to have been a king of that name in Ś. 380, *i.e.* 458 A.D.

Dr. Fleet has assigned the date of about 500 A.D., to the Penugoṇḍa plates, which is the date we give to (26) Skandavarman, son of (25) Siṁhavarman who crowned king Mâdhava II *alias* Siṁhavarman.

The name Siṁhavarman given to a king of the western Gaṅga dynasty shows that Âryavarman who had been crowned by the Pallava King (25) Siṁhavarman had married his daughter and his son Madhava II. received the name of his grandfather, the Pallava king Siṁhavarman.

The Vâyalûr inscription enables us to believe that the Penugoṇḍa plates belong to about 500 A.D.

In the Vâyalûr list, the predecessor of Siṁhavishṇu is called Siṁhavarman, and this name is engraved very clearly. This is a remarkable fact, since it confirms what is stated in verse 10 of the Vêlûrpâḷaiyam plates.

« Then from the king named Siṁhavarman, who wiped off » the pride of (his) enemies, was born the victorious Siṁhavishṇu » whose prowess was widely known on earth.»

If we admit : 1° the identity of (19) Vishṇugôpa with the adversary of Samudragupta in A. D. 338—and, 2° the identity of (21) Skandavarman with Skandavarman (I), of the Ômgôḍu No. 1 plates, we obtain the following chronology :

Vâyalûr	Vishṇugôpa	A. D.	338
	Vishṇudâsa (Kumâravishṇu)	„	366
Ômgôḍu No. 1.	Skandavarman (I)	„	394
	Vîravarman	„	422
	Skandavarman (II)	„	450
Chûra	(Y. M.) Vishṇugôpa	„	478
	Siṁhavarman	„	506
Vâyalûr	Vishṇugôpa	„	534
	Siṁhavarman	„	562
	Siṁhavishṇu	„	590
	Mahêndravarman I.	„	618
	Narasiṁhavarman I	„	646

It is not necessary, in conclusion, to say what a flood of light the deciphering of the Vâyalûr inscription has thrown on the history of the early Pallavas: the importance of the inscription is naturally very great as it gives us the most ancient and complete list of kings.

CHAPTER III.

TELUGU ORIGIN OF THE MAHÊNDRAVARMAN STYLE.

The deciphering of the Vâyalûr inscription has led us to think that the genealogy of the predecessors of Siṁhavishṇu stood thus:

(29) Siṁhavarman
|
(30) Vishṇugôpa
|
(31) Siṁhavarman
|
(32) Siṁhavishṇu.

It is certain that the father of Siṁhavishṇu was (31) Siṁhavarman who seems to have been so named after his grandfather, (29) Siṁhavarman. Again we have admitted the identification of (30) Vishṇugôpa with the one who granted the Chûra plates, from Palakkada. It is also highly probable that (29) Siṁhavarman, the donor of the No. 2 Ôṁgôdu, Pikîra and Mâṅgaḷûr plates was not king of Kâñchî but reigned in the districts of Nellore and Guntûr. From this we have to conclude that the direct ancestors of Siṁhavishṇu and Mahêndravarman lived perhaps in the Telugu country. We shall now proceed to show the importance of this detail.

When, last year, I wrote the first volume of "Pallava Antiquities", I was struck by the fact that king Mahêndra-Vikrama whose inscriptions I copied at Pallâvaram (*Pall. Ant.*, Vol. I, Plate XXI, A.) and at Trichinopoly (*Pall. Ant.*, Vol. I, Plate XXIII.) and who in all probability cut the caves containing these inscriptions had many surnames; such as Chivibhunduṇḍu, Nilvilônayyambu, Ventulavittu, Pasarambu, etc., which seem to be all of Telugu origin. Those who have studied the inscriptions at Trichinopoly (Archæological Survey of India—Annual Report for 1903-4, p. 271) and at Pallâvaram (*G. O.*, No. 538, 28th July 1909—Part II, No. 14, p. 75), have mentioned this fact, but they have not drawn any conclusion from it.

I believe that Mahêndravarman I. had names of Telugu origin because he or his father perhaps reigned over the Telugu country.

Now the following important question presents itself: What was at the time of the Pallavas the line of demarcation between the Tamil and the Telugu countries?

Epigraphy has furnished an answer to this question:

« It is worthy of note that the earlier inscriptions at Tondama-
» nâd, Kâḷahasti, Guḍimallam, Tirupati, Tiruchchâṉûr and Yôgi-
» Mallavaram in the North Arcot district are in Tamil, though the
» prevailing language is at present Telugu. The same was the
» case at Nellore in the 12th and 13th centuries. We may, there-
» fore, conclude that the tract comprising these villages and the
» southern portion of the Nellore district was originally Tamil
» country and the change of language into Telugu probably began
» during Vijayanagara times. » (*G. O.*, Nos. 678, 679, 12th Aug. 1914, p. 7).

From the above, it follows, that at the time of the Pallavas the region now forming the Nellore district served as the frontier between the Tamil and the Telugu countries.

We have therefore to conclude that we find Telugu names in the caves of Mahêndra because either Siṁhavishṇu or Mahêndra himself reigned over the country lying to the north of the modern town of Nellore. In Vol. I. of 'Pallava Antiquities' I have said that in the Tamil country there is not a single antiquity which could with certainty be attributed to the time anterior to that of Mahêndra; I have therefore been led to think that it was this king who, by his own initiative, spread in the Tamil country a taste for sculpture in general and rock-cut temples in particular.

But whence did Mahêndravarman himself get this taste for temples sculptured in rocks?

The reply can be easily found if we take the two preceding propositions together. As Mahêndra reigned in the Telugu country it was probably in the banks of the Kṛishṇâ that he acquired a taste for rock-cut temples; and so the Pallava Art of the time of Mahêndravarman had its origin in the Telugu country.

It is but a hypothesis, but a hypothesis that can be verified by studying the art that flourished in the VI century on the banks of the Kṛishṇâ. It is certain that this art existed: There are rock-cut temples at Bezwada and at Mogulrazapuram on the northern bank of the Kṛishṇâ; and on the southern bank there are the temples of Sittanavasal and Undavalli. It must however be admitted that this art has remained quite unknown up to the present: only, the Undavalli temple has been described not very distinctly but in such a manner that it is impossible to form a correct idea of the style of those sculptures.

For these reasons I thought it necessary to go and see the caves on the banks of the Kṛishṇâ and particularly the temple of Anantaśayana at Undavalli.

We know that this temple does not contain any very ancient inscription and that the age of this monument can be ascertained only from its architectural style.

And the authors who have handled this subject hold such different opinions that it is very difficult to arrive at a decision on this matter.

Sir Walter Elliot (*Ind. Ant.*, Vol. V, p. 80) was struck by the resemblance they bore to the sculptures at Mahâbalipuram; but there he speaks only of the general impression; this author does not seem to have made a minute study of these monuments; at all events, he gives no arguments in support of his thesis.

Mr. Sewell (List of *Antiquities*, Vol. I, p. 77) is of opinion that it is the work of the Châlukyas. And M. R. Ry. H. Krishna Sastri who visited these caves on the 20th and the 28th December 1908 says very correctly that it does not seem to be the work of the Châlukyas, because, not a single cave is known to have been dug by them (*G. O.*, No. 538, 28th July 1909, Part II, No. 13, p. 74).

He remarks a resemblance with the Pallava sculptures: « The ornamental designs on the tops of four of the niches in this » hall resemble very much those on the "Rathas" at Mahâbali- » puram. »

M. R. Ry. H. Krishna Sastri remarks, however, certain points of resemblance with the caves of Orissa and thinks that the temple at Undavalli « might have come into existence in the » Ândhra period. »

Thus we see that the opinions of the various authors differ much. Mr. H. Krishna Sastri attributes these sculptures to the Ândhra period, *i.e.*, the I or II century of the Christian era; Mr. R. Sewell, on the contrary, dates them in the VII or the VIII century. From this we may conclude that a general impression will not do for fixing the age of these sculptures and that only a most attentive study of the minutest details of ornamentation can lead to any adequate result.

In 1912 I visited the caves of Bâdâmi which are the works of the ancient Châlukyas. I examined the style of these temples very attentively and have given my impressions about them in my book (*Archéologie du Sud de l'Inde*, Tome I, Architecture, ps. 173, 174, 175 and Pl. CLVIII, B). The style of these caves differs entirely from the Pallava style and there is no resemblance between them. Again, the old theory that the Chalukyan artists were the authors of the Pallava temples cannot at all be admitted and I do not believe that anybody will dream of maintaining it to-day.

It was not without curiosity that I visited the Undavalli caves. What was the style of these sculptures and what did they resemble? The Ândhra or the Châlukya or the Pallava style?

What was my surprise when I stood before those sculptures at Undavalli! *The Undavalli sculptures belong entirely and even in the minutest details to the style of Mahêndravarman.*

We have given a description of this style in Chapter II, Vol. I of "*Pallava Antiquities*"; and the resemblance between the caves of Mahêndra and those at Undavalli is so complete that there is no difference to be pointed out.

The plans are the same. The principal cave at Undavalli is a four-storied one. The ground-floor and the top floor remain all unfinished. The last story but one where the image of Ananta-śayana (Vishṇu lying on a serpent) is placed, is also left unfinished. There is thus but one story that has been completed. Here the plan is very simple: they are three caves of Mahêndra placed beside one another.

The middle cave is almost in the same plan as the rock-cut temple at Pallâvaram (*Pall. Ant.*, Vol. I, Plate XX). The right and the left caves have the same plan as the Maṇḍagapattu cave (*Pall. Ant.*, Vol. I, p. 56) and the left cave at Mâmandûr.

Besides, there are many other caves in this very rock at Undavalli; they are almost all of them in ruins but their plan is easily ascertained. It is the very simple one used in all the temples cut in the rock during the time of Mahêndra.

The pillars belong to the well-known type represented in Plates IX, XII, XIII, XV, XVI, XIX, XXI, XXVII, XXVIII, XXIX of Vol. I, of "*Pallava Antiquities*". They are square in section and adorned with lotus flowers as at Mahêndravâdi and Dalavânûr. The Dvârapâlas resemble neither those of the temples of Rājasiṁha nor those of Mahâbalipuram. They are like those found in the caves of Mahéndra. Some of them have their hand raised in sign of adoration as at Tirukkalukkunṛam (*Pall. Ant.*, Vol. I, Plate XXVI), at Singavaram, at Mâmandûr and at Dalavânûr (*Pall. Ant.*, Vol. I, Plate XVI, B). But most of them rest it on a club with the same pose that we have noticed at Trichinopoly (*Pall. Ant.*, Vol. I., Pl. XXII), at Vallam (*Pall. Ant.*, Vol I., Pl. VIII) and at other places: Dalavânûr, Mandagapattu, Tirukkalukkunṛam, Mâmandûr, Sîyamangalam, etc.

The niches are ornamented with a very special kind of framework that we have noticed at Dalavânûr (*Pall. Ant.*, Vol. I., Pl. XVI,) and at Sîyamangalam (*Pall. Ant.*, Vol. I., Pl. XVIII) and which we have called 'double-arched tiruvatchi' (Torana).

The shrines are empty—as elsewhere in most of the temples of Mahêndra—but there exist on the right side of the temple at Undavalli certain niches that contain lingams.

At Undavalli we find kûdus with the head of Gandharva resembling those seen in the Pallava temples (vide the kûdus of Dalavânûr represented in *Pall. Ant.*, Vol. I, Pl. XVI, A.)

The floors of these temples are ornamented outside with pavilions resembling those at Mahâbalipuram; they are the "Karṇakûḍu" and the "Śâlai" like those represented in Fig. 23 of our work on "Dravidian Architecture."

Besides, the small niches, mentioned above, which are found to the right of the façade, are but small "Rathas". They exactly resemble the small shrine seen in the middle of the bas-relief, "Bhagiratha's penance," at Mahâbalipuram. The style of architecture is identically the same.

All the authors that have spoken of the temple at Undavalli have believed that it was dedicated to Vishṇu; it is not so. No doubt the Vishṇu cult occupies a predominant place there but there are also many shrines dedicated to Śiva. We have already said that the small "Rathas" to the right of the façade contain lingams.

The principal image in the temple is indeed that of Anantaśayana; but this image is found also in the temples of Śiva.

At Mahâbalipuram in particular, the bas-relief representing Vishṇu lying on the serpent is not in a temple of Vishṇu. It is found in the cave near the light-house which was undoubtedly dedicated to Śiva; god Anantaśayana is represented in the same form both at Undavalli and Mahâbalipuram. Unfortunately at Undavalli almost the whole of the body of the god has disappeared; it may be due either to the wear and tear of time or to the iconoclastic work of the Mussulmans. The image we now find there, is a rough figure made of cement. However, a close examination of it shows that at one time the god had his arm stretched out as at Mahâbalipuram and Singavaram.

In short, the caves of Undavalli differ completely from those of Bâdâmi and resemble much those of the Pallavas.

However they are not exactly like those of Mahâbalipuram: Nowhere do we see the squatting lions supporting the pillars [we have said that these squatting lions should have been an invention of the artists of the epoch of Narasiṁhavarman I.]; the Dvârapâlas at Undavalli do not resemble those of Mahâbalipuram.

On the contrary, the sculptures of Undavalli very much resemble those of the caves of Mahêndra.

(*a*) The plan of the caves is the same.

(*b*) The pillars have cubical parts ornamented with lotus flowers.

(*c*) The doors and the niches have a kind of framework which is different from the 'doubled-arched tiruvatchi'.

(*d*) The Dvarapâlas have the same pose.

In short, the caves of Undavalli belong to the style of Mahêndra.

We have said above, that, during many centuries, many generations of Pallava kings had reigned over the country near the banks of the Kṛishṇâ in the districts of Guntûr and Nellore. We have also observed that the caves of Trichinopoly and Pallâvaram contain the surnames of Mahêndra which are all of Telugu origin and we have supposed that Mahêndravarman I reigned over the Telugu country and imported into the Tamil country the art that existed on the banks of the Kṛishṇâ.

Undavalli is in the Guntûr taluq of the Guntûr district. The caves are situated on the southern bank of the Kṛishṇâ. In the absence of any inscription enabling us to know the origin of these caves, we might suppose that they are the work of the Pallavas who reigned over this country before it was conquered by the Châlukyas.

Well, that is not my opinion.

I do not think that the caves of Undavalli were dug by the Pallavas. On closely examining the sculptures, I have made a discovery which I believe will prove to be of great importance in ascertaining the origin of these temples.

On the cubical portion forming the foot of two of the pillars I have found the image of lions (Fig. 1).

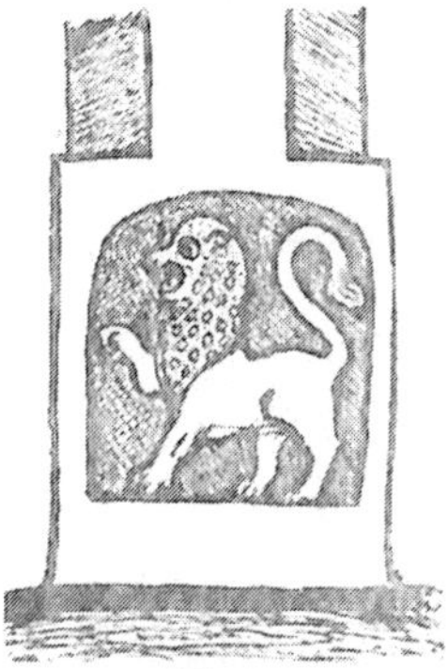

Fig. 1.
A lion (simha) at Undavalli.

At the foot of another pillar I have observed the image of a vase.

It is true that these lions resemble very much those of Śîyamangalam, an image of which is given in Vol. I. of Pallava Antiquities (Pl. XIX).

Lastly certain coins bearing the images of a lion and a vase have been attributed to the Pallavas (vide Vincent A. Smith's Early History of India, Plate facing p. 1).

It would therefore be possible to use this argument to affirm that the caves of Undavalli are the work of the Pallavas.

My opinion, which is quite different, is *that the Caves of Undavalli are the work of the Vishnukundins.*

There is no doubt that this dynasty reigned on the banks of the Godavary and the Kṛishṇâ before that country was conquered by the Châlukyas. The village of Peruvâḍaka in the district of Pḻaki-râshṭra, which belonged to the Vishṇukuṇḍins at the time when Indravarman granted the Râmatîrtham plates (*Ep. Ind.*, Vol. XII., No. 17, p. 133), passed into the hands of the Châlukyan king Vishṇuvardhana I. while he was still a vassal of Pulakêśin II. (Timmapuram plates—*Ep. Ind.*, Vol. IX., p. 317).

The Vishṇukuṇḍins were therefore the predecessors of the Châlukyas in the Vengi country. One of their capitals was Lenduḷûru (Dendulûru in the Ellore taluq). The cradle of this family was probably Viṅukoṇḍa in the Kṛishṇâ district. They were fervent worshippers of the god at Śrîparvata (Śriśailam) in the Kurnool district.

As it is certain that the Eastern Châlukyas reigned in the Guntûr district when Sarvalôkâśrâya granted the village of Chandalûr in 673 A.D. (*Ep. Ind.*, Vol. VIII, No. 24), we may affirm that the Vishṇukuṇḍins reigned before this epoch, probably towards the end of the VI century.

From our point of view, the Chikkula plates (*Ep. Ind.*, Vol. IV, No. 25, p. 195) are very interesting.

1° The seal represents a lion exactly like the one we have remarked at Undavalli. The Chikkula seal is represented in *Ep. Ind.*, Vol. IV., to face page 244. This seal is analogous to the Râmatîrtham plates which M. R. Ry. H. Krishna Sastri has described as follows:

« An advancing lion or tiger with its left fore-paw raised, its neck erect, mouth wide open and the tail swung over the back so as to end in a loop. (*G. O.*, No. 538, 28th July 1909).»

It must be noted that coins bearing a lion and a vase are found on the banks of the Godavary and the Kṛishṇâ; and I am convinced that they do not belong to the Pallavas but to the Vishṇukuṇḍins.

2° The village gifted away by these plates is Rêgonṛam which is situated to the south-east of the village of Râvirêva on the bank of the Kṛishṇâ: « Rêgonṛam, which was south-east of the village of Rêvirêva on the bank of the Kṛishṇâ beṇṇa, *i.e.*, the river Kṛishṇâ.».

So it is beyond all doubt that the Vishṇukuṇḍins reigned on the banks of the Kṛishṇâ.

3° The following genealogy is found in these plates:

Mâdhavavarman
|
Vikramêndravarman I.
|
Indrabhaṭṭârakavarman
|
Vikramêndravarman II.

We know also that the mother of Vikramêndravarman I. belonged to the family of Vâkâṭakas. Indeed, it has been said of Vikramêndravarman I. that his « birth was embellished by the two families of the Vishṇukuṇḍins and Vâkâṭakas.».

On the other hand, a donation of the Vishṇukuṇḍins discovered in 1914 (No. 7 of Appendix A., *G. O.* No. 920, 4th Aug. 1914—Part II, No. 35) shows that the name Vikramêndra is a corrupted form of Vikramahêndra.

If we remember, then, that in the Śiyamaṅgalam cave there is the image of a lion resembling the one found in the seal of the Chikkula plates, that the Undavalli sculptures resemble those of the Pallava caves, that Undavalli stands on the banks of the Kṛishṇâ where the Vishṇukuṇḍins had reigned, and that the inscriptions of Mahêndravarman I. at Trichinopoly and at Pallâvaram contain Telugu epithets, we shall be struck with these coincidences.

But there is another point of coincidence. Among the Pallava kings that have reigned before Siṁhavishṇu, there is not one named Mahêndra. It would appear that this name was not hereditary in the Pallava family and that Mahêndravarman I. was really the first king of that name.

The account given of the Vâyalûr inscription in the report on Epigraphy for 1908-09 mentions Mahêndravarman (once) among the 25 predecessors of Siṁhavishṇu. Now that the Vâyalûr inscription is completely deciphered, it is manifest that that name is not there, but we find the name (6) Chandravarman. Perhaps it is the ending "ndravarman" that led to the reading [Mahê]ndravarman.

In the Trichinopoly and Pallâvaram inscriptions this king is called Mahêndra-Vikrama. But then, there were Vishṇukuṇḍin kings who bore the name of Vikramahêndra.

In my opinion, these coincidences can all be explained in a very simple manner: The Pallavas at the end of the VI century reigned in the districts of Nellore and Guntûr; their neighbours were the Vishṇukuṇḍins who reigned on the banks of the Kṛishṇâ; Siṁhavishṇu married probably the daughter of a Vishṇukuṇḍin king named Vikramahêndra and gave his son the name of his grand-father, Mahêndravikrama.

We know that Vikramêndravarman I. was the son of a Vâkâtaka princess; and the inscriptions of the Vâkâtaka kings are found engraved in the caves of Ajanta. It is probable that it was owing to their Vâkâtaka origin that the Vishṇukuṇḍins had the idea of digging caves on the banks of the Kṛishṇâ—caves that we see even now at Bezwada, Mogulrazapuram, Undavalli and Sittanagaram. The Pallava king Mahêndravarman I, who was the grand-son of a Vishṇukuṇḍin king, having had many occasions to admire those caves that had been dug by his relatives, had similar ones cut on the rock around Kâñchîpuram.

CHAPTER IV.

THE DYNASTY OF SIMHAVISHNU.

§ I.—The Vêlûrpâḷaiyam plates coupled with the Vâyalûr inscription inform us that Siṁhavishṇu was the son of (31) Siṁhavarman.

The Vêlûrpâḷaiyam plates say of Siṁhavishṇu :

« He quickly seized the country of the Chôḷas embellished by » the daughter of Kavîra (*i.e.* the river Kâvêrî), whose ornaments » are the forests of paddy (fields) and where (are found) brilliant » groves of areca (palms).»

From this it would appear that the Chôḷa country did not belong to the Pallavas before Siṁhavishṇu and that it was he who conquered it.

This military operation was perhaps difficult, for it seems that all the southern kings opposed it : the Kâśâkuḍi plates say, indeed, that Siṁhavishṇu vanquished « The Malaya, Kaḷabhra, » Mâlava, Chôḷa and Pâṇḍya (kings), the Siṁhala (king) who was » proud of the strength of his arms, and the Kêraḷas.»

§ II.—Mahêndravarman I. is the first king about whom we have precise information.

It is probable that Mahêndra gained a victory at Puḷḷalûra [according to the Kâśâkuḍi plates]. It is thought that this town can be identified with Pullalûr (Chingleput District—Conjeeveram taluk) which is at a distance of 15 miles north of Kâñchî. No one knows for certain who was his adversary ; it is supposed it was Pulakêśin II.

The Aihole inscription (*Ep. Ind.*, Vol. VI, No. 1, p. 11) praises Pulakêśin thus :

(V. 29) « .... He caused the splendour of the lord of the » Pallavas, who had opposed the rise of his power, to be obscured » by the dust of his army, and to vanish behind the walls of » Kâñchîpura.

(V. 30) « When straightway he strove to conquer the Chôḷas, » the Kâvêrî, who has the darting corps for her tremulous eyes, had » her current obstructed by the causeway formed by his elephants » whose rutting-juice was dripping down, and avoided the contact » with the ocean.

(V. 31) « There he caused great prosperity to the Chôḷas, » Kêraḷas and Pâṇḍyas, he being the hot-rayed sun to the hoar- » frost—the army of the Pallavas.»

We have said in the preceding chapter that the country lying between the towns of Ellore and Guntûr probably formed part of the kingdom of Mahêndra.

Again, it is certain, that, in the middle of the VII century, this country belonged to the Châlukyas.

It is, therefore, likely that Pulakêśin II conquered it about 610 A.D., *i.e.*, at the beginning of the reign of Mahêndravarman I.

The latter, thus dispossessed of the northern provinces of his kingdom, lived in the Tamil country during the latter part of his reign and it was then he encouraged the arts of that country as we shall presently show.

In Pallava Antiquities (Vol. I. p. 40), we have admitted with V. Venkayya (*Ep. Ind.*, Vol. III, p. 277) that Mahêndra who was first a Jain, was converted to the Siva cult by saint Appar (Sékkiḻâr's Periapurânam, Madras, 1870); we have also said, though without any positive proof, yet, owing to our moral conviction, that it was Mahêndravarman I. who was the author of the rock-cut temples that we have described in Chapter II. of the aforesaid book.

In the course of this year (1916-17) we have learnt much more about Mahêndravarman I.

In "*Pallava Antiquities*" Vol. I., I have spoken about the right side cave at Mâmandûr (ps. 53, 54, 55,). Judging from the style of Architecture, I have attributed this cave to Mahêndra-varman I. and have described the inscription found there in the following terms: « Mr. E. Hultzsch who mentions this inscription » (No. 38— *G. O.*, No. 424, 20th April 1888), declares that it is » "illegible". However, one important remark has to be made » here: the alphabet is identically the same as that of Mahêndra- » vâdi. Pl. XXVII, B. is a photograph of a small part of the » inscription which will enable us to judge of the form of the » characters.»

So then, relying on :

1° the style of architecture,

2° the palæography of the inscriptions,

I concluded that this cave must be attributed to Mahêndravarman I.

When I examined the inscription, it seemed to me that, though it was very much damaged, it would perhaps be possible to make something out of it.

Mr. Hultzsch, when he copied it, did not understand it, but that is not a reason why it should be abandoned for ever.

I believed that a more attentive study of it might enable us to obtain some interesting information.

So, in January 1917, I went to Mâmandûr to copy the inscription.

This labour was well rewarded:

In the midst of many incomprehensible phrases I read the words: " Mattavilâsâdipadamprahasana " (see Pl. III, A). I did not understand their meaning; but I was at once struck with the name Mattavilâsa which is a name of Mahêndravarman I. that I have seen engraved in the caves of Trichinopoly and Pallâvaram (*Pall. Ant.*, Vol. I, p. 39); and I was glad to have discovered a new proof of what I had asserted in attributing the Mâmandûr cave to Mahêndravarman I.

I sent a copy of the Mâmandûr inscription to M.R.Ry. T. A. Gopinatha Rao requesting him to tell me what he made out of it.

A few days after, I received from him an article which he had published in February 1917 in the " Madras Christian College Magazine " which mentioned the following important discovery:

" Paṇḍit T. Gaṇapati Śâstri," the curator of Śaṅskṛit Manuscripts, Travancore, has very recently discovered a manuscript called " Mattavilâsa-prahasana ".

What is very remarkable is that the author of this Saṅskṛit poem is a king named Mahêndravarman. It is specified that this king belonged to the dynasty of the Pallavas of Kâñchî, that he was the son of Siṁhavishṇu, and that he had the surnames of: Avanibhâjana, Mattavilâsa, Guṇabhara, Śatrumalla.

As soon as I received this communication I replied to M. R. Ry. T. A. Gopinatha Rao by a letter dated 12th April informing him that I was very pleased with the discovery he brought to the notice of the public and that, in my opinion, the

Plate III.

A.
Mâmandûr
cave insc.

B
Kûram
Siva temple
inscription,

C.
Kânchipuram
Airâvatêsvara
temple insc.

words that I had read at the end of the 6th line of the Mâmandûr inscription seemed to confirm the fact that the poet king Mahêndravarman I. was the author of the earliest rock-cut temples. Besides, as the musical inscription at Kuḍumiyamalai (*Ep. Ind.*, Vol. XII, p. 226) is written in an alphabet resembling that of Tṛichinopoly (*Pall. Ant.*, Vol I, Pl. XXIII), we may suppose that Mahêndravarman I. was also a musician.

Mr. Gopinatha Rao in his reply dated 19th April said:

« No doubt the discovery of the burlesque Mattavilâsa-
» prahasana is important; but what is more important is the
» mention of this work very definitely in the mutilated inscription
» of Mâmaṇḍûr............The musical composition discovered and
» copied for the Epigraphist's office by me [at Kudumiyamalai],
» is not a composition of Mahêndravarman though it belongs no
» doubt to the same period. It was composed by one Rudrâchârya.
» No doubt in the Annual Report Venkayya says:

» The inscription was apparently engraved at the instance of
» an unnamed king, who was a disciple of a certain Rudrâcharya
» and who composed these "svaras" for the benefit of his pupils.
» We may only suspect if the unnamed king be not Mahêndra-
» varman, but cannot be sure of it.»

And in a letter dated 28th April, he added:

« The [Mâmaṇḍûr] inscription seems to refer to "svaras" and
» "varṇas" of Music,—is your surmise that the Kuḍimiyâmalai
» Musical record was engraved at the instance of Mahêndra going
» to be true?—talks of *Kavis* (poets), mentions Vâlmîki and the
» Matavilâsaprahasana. As suspected by you, the record perhaps
» gives a panegyric on the literary and musical talents of the
» Pallava king Mahêndravarman.»

The village of Mahêndramaṅgalam in the subdivision of Mâvaṇḍûrpparṟil mentioned in the inscription No. 41 of 1890 on the store-room (northern wall) of the Vardhamâna Temple at Tirupparuttikkuṉṟu (*Ep. Ind.*, Vol. VII, No. 15, p. 115) has certainly been named after Mahêndravarman I.

The tank at Mâmandûr was named Çitramêga, probably after a "biruda" of Mahêndra.

The discovery of the similarity of architectural style existing between the caves of Mahêndra and those at Undavalli and the other discovery that in the Mâmandûr cave there is mention of Mattavilâsaprahasana,—these two discoveries taken along with others enable us to conclude that King Mahêndravarman I. is one of the greatest figures in the history of Tamilian civilisation.

1° From a military point of view, he has checked at Pullalûr the invasion of the Châlukyas.

2° As for religion, he has given a new impulse to Saivism.

3° As for the arts, being himself a royal artist, he has glorified poetry and music.

4° As for the plastic art, he has transported the taste for rock-cut temples from the banks of the Kṛishṇâ to those of the Pâlar and the Kâvêrî.

5° As for the administration, he built the tanks at Mahêndravâdi, Mâmandûr, and probably also at Dalavânûr.

Mahêndravarman I. has opened a new era whose apotheosis we shall see in the reign of his son Narasiṁhavarman the Great.

§ III.—In 640, the Chinese pilgrim Hiuen Tsang stayed at Kâñchîpuram and it is probable that this year falls within the reign of Narasiṁhavarman I. The chronology of the Châlukyas says indeed that it was about 642 that this king took possession of Vâtâpi (Bâdâmi).

The Kûram plates (*S.I.I.*, Vol I., p. 152) give us information about this event. They say first that Narasiṁhavarman I. vanquished Pulakêśin in the battles of Pariyaḷa, Maṇimaṅgala, Śuramâra, etc. Probably Maṇimaṅgala is nothing but Manimangalam (Saidapet taluk, Chingleput district) which is at a distance of 20 miles from Kâñchî. In that case it would appear that the Tamil country was invaded a second time by the same Châlukyan king. For the second time Pulakêśin II. was repulsed by the Pallavas. The glorious Châlukyan emperor who had vanquished Harsha Vardhana and whose friendship had been sought by the King of Persia was thoroughly routed and his capital Vâtâpi was destroyed.

In regard to this last point, all documents (Kûram, Kâśâkuḍi, Udayendiram, etc.) agree. The Vêlûrpâḷaiyam plates add also a detail: Narasiṁhavarman (I) « took (from his enemies) the pillar » of victory standing in the centre of (the town of) Vâtâpi » (*S.I.I.*, Vol. II, part v., p. 511). This fact is confirmed by the inscription at Bâdâmi (*Ind. Ant.*, Vol IX) the alphabet of which is the same as that of the Pallavas and which mentions Narasiṁhavishṇu, alias Mahâmalla as also a commemorative column (Jayastambha)

Speaking of Narasiṁhavarman I., the Kâśâkuḍi plates say: « Who surpassed the glory of the valour of Râma by (his) conquest of Laṅkâ »

This event is confirmed by the Chronicles of Ceylon (Translation of the Mahâvaṁsa by Wijesinha) and it took place after 642 A.D., because, according to these chronicles, the Singhalese prince Mâṇavamma aided Narasiṁha in repulsing Vallabha (Pulakêśin) and the two expeditions to Ceylon took place only after that.

It was perhaps during these expeditions that Narasiṁha vanquished the Chôḷas, Keralas, Kaḷabhras and Paṇḍyas as mentioned in the Kûram plates.

It is probable that the navy took part in the conquest of Ceylon, for the Mahâvaṁsa says that Mâṇavamma crossed the sea in ships.

We may suppose that the port of Mâmallapuram served as the naval station for the Pallava fleet. Even now Mahâbalipuram serves as a landmark for all vessels.

In the first volume of *Pallava Antiquities* I have proved that the monuments at Mahâbalipuram do not belong to the style of Mahêndra, that this town did not probably exist before the time of Narasiṁhavarman I., and that it is this king that founded it and and gave it the name of Mahâmallapuram after his own name of Mâmalla and began the cutting of the "Rathas" and "Caves" there.

I am convinced that in the year 650 A.D., the sculpturing of the rocks of Mahâbalipuram was being executed.

The second expedition to Ceylon was crowned with success; the Pallava army conquered Ceylon; and Mâṇavamma cut off the head of King Hattha-datta II.

In what year was Ceylon conquered? Since we know that after the capture of Bâdâmi there were two expeditions to this island, this conquest probably took place several years after 642 A.D., and I would put it after 650 A.D.

The chronology of Mahâvaṁsa affirms that the death of Hattha-dâta and the coronation of Mâṇavamma took place in 691 A.D. What value are we to attach to this information?

I think we may affirm that for the X century (900 A.D.—1000 A.D.) the chronology of Mahâvaṁsa is very correct but on condition that the dates are all reduced by 24 years.

Does this rule apply to the VII century ? If we take away 24 years from 691, we get 667, *i.e.*, 17 years more than 650.

We have said that Ceylon was conquered perhaps after 650, but it appears that it was less than 17 years after that date.

I think that the following hypotheses may be admitted :

1° Ceylon was conquered about 660 A.D., at the end of the reign of Narasiṁhavarman I.

2° The chronology of Mahâvaṁsa is accurate enough provided we reduce the dates by nearly a quarter of a century.

We shall have occasion later on to utilise this result.

§ IV.—The reign of Mahêndravarman II, was probably short and uneventful. The Kûram plates, dated in the time of his son, only say that his reign was prosperous and that he was a legislator « who thoroughly enforced the sacred law of the castes and the orders ».

§ V.—The Kûram plates give a long description of the military exploits of Paramêśvaravarman I. and also mention the name of his royal adversary: « He made Vikramâditya, whose » army consisted of several lakshas, take to flight, covered only » by a rag.».

On the other hand the Udayêndiram plates (*S.I.I.*, Vol. II, Part III, p. 371) give us the name of the battle: « Paramêśvara- » varman, who defeated the army of Vallabha in the battle of » Peruvaḷanallûr ».

An extremely important detail, which, in my opinion, has not so far been noted well, is the date of the conflict between Paramêśvaravarman I. (called Ugradaṇḍa and Lokâditya in the inscriptions of the Kailâsanâtha temple at Kâñchîpuram, *S.I.I.*, Vol. I.) and Vikramâditya I. (Raṇarasika).

From 1910, we have been in possession of a document which gives this date with great certitude,—I mean the Gadval plates. This grant (*Ep. Ind.*, Vol. X, No. 22, p. 101) has been made when Vikramâditya I. was encamped in the Chôḷa kingdom on the southern bank of the Kâvêrî.

Besides, they bear the date of the year of the reign and of the Śaka era. The exact date is incontestably 674 A.D.

We shall now proceed to determine a second point of very great importance.

Mr. Hultzsch who edited these plates has said :

« When Vikramâditia made this grant, his army had invaded » the Chôḷikavishaya, *i.e.*, the Chôḷa province, and was encamped » in Uragapura on the southern bank of the Kâvêrî river (l. 25 f.). » In sending me the impressions, Mr. Venkayya drew my atten- » tion to the fact that Uragapura is mentioned in Kâlidâsa's » Raghuvaṁśa (vi. 59) as the capital of the Pâṇḍya king, and » proposed to identify it with the ancient Chôḷa capital Uṟaiyûr » near Trichinopoly; I rather think that Uragapura, "the snake- » city" is a poetical equivalent of Nâgapattanam (now Nega- » patam) ....».

But, I believe that Mr. Hultzsch is entirely mistaken.

In connection with this subject I have made a discovery which appears to me to be decisive: I have spotted the village of Peruvalanallûr where was fought the battle between Paramêśvaravarman I. and Vikramâditya. This village is in the Trichinopoly Taluq of the district of the same name, on the left bank of the Kâvêrî, and at a distance of 10 miles north-west of Trichinopoly.

I am of opinion that it is not possible to doubt that the town of Uragapuram where Vikramâditya I. was encamped is any other place than Uṟaiyur (Trichinopoly).

In the inscription of Râjasiṁha found at the base of the Vimâna of Kailâsanâtha temple at Kâñchîpuram (*S.I.I.*, Vol. I. p. 13) Paramêśvara is named « Ugradaṇḍa the destroyer of the city of Raṇarasika ». It is to be noted that in the Gadval plates the surname of "Raṇarasika" is given to Vikramâditya. But which is the town designated by the words « the city of Raṇarasika »?

I do not think it could be Bâdâmî, for, in that case, Paramêśvara would not have failed to assume, as his grand-father, the title of "Vâtâpikoṇḍa".

I believe that "the town of Raṇarasika" is Uragapuram (Uṟaiyur).

The Gadval grant which was made when Vikramâditya was encamped at Trichinopoly gives us a detailed description which is very life-like of the third invasion of the Châlukyas into the Tamil country.

The Pallavas are called there "The family of Mâmalla" (verse 5).

How did Paramêśvaravarman I. succeed in repulsing the Châlukyas?

The Kêndûr plates (*Ep. Ind.*. Vol. IX, No. 29, p. 205) tell us that the Châlukyas had to contend against the Pâṇḍyas, the Chôḷas, the Kêraḷas, the Kaḷabhras and the kings of Kavêra, Pârasîka, Siṁhaḷa. It is therefore probable that all the people of the south combined together against the invaders. The aforesaid plates themselves say that there was a confederation of three kings. One of these was perhaps the king of Kâñchî. Maṉavamma, the king of Siṁhaḷa, was probably another. The Mahâvaṁsa says that this king reigned 35 years. We have said that he ascended the throne about 660 A.D. So he must have surely reigned in 674 A.D. He had been Minister to Narasiṁhavarman I. and he was perhaps attached to Paramêśvaravarman I. by ties of friendship. If our suppositions are correct, by 674 A.D., only 14 years would have passed since he ascended the throne with the aid of the Pallavas. And at a time when the latter were in danger it was his duty to act according to the dictates of the simplest feelings of gratefulness.

The third king that entered the coalition against the Châlukyas was probably the king of the Pâṇḍyas. We shall refer to this question again when we examine the history of the Pâṇḍyas later on.

It is certain that Paramêśvaravarman lived some time after the defeat of Vikramâditya, for the Kûram plates are posterior to this event, but unfortunately they are not dated.

The object of the Kûram record (*S.S.I.*, Vol. I., p. 154) is a gift made to the temple of Śiva called Vidyâvinîta-Pallava-Paramêśvara which had been built at Kûram by Vidyâvinîta-Pallava.

There is a temple of Śiva now at Kûram. The Epigraphical Department have copied an inscription of Nandivarman Maharâja found in this temple (No. 38 of 1900); the writing seems to belong to the IX century, but they have not found any inscription which could be attributed to the epoch of Paramêśvaravarman I.

When I visited this place, I discovered an inscription which has not been mentioned by any one till now. I do not know how it has escaped investigation so long, seeing that it is well preserved and the letters are all cut fair and deep. This inscription which is reproduced in Plate III, is the following:

Text:

ஸ்ரீ பல்லவ
மாராசன்

Śrî-Pallava-Mârâsaṉ.

The name of the king is not given, but the alphabet employed leaves no doubt as to the antiquity of the inscription. The letters 'Śrî' and 'va', in particular, are so formed that we may say that the inscription belongs to the VII century.

So, the Śiva temple at Kûram is certainly the Vidyâvinîta-Pallava-Paramêśvara temple mentioned in the plates, but alas! in what a dilapidated condition! No doubt the adjoining maṇḍapam has been rebuilt with the old stones. As for the sanctuary itself, only the ground-work remains, which, however, enables us to know two important facts :

1° The temple was apsidal in form as the Sâhadêvaratha at Mahâbalipuram.

2° The entrance into the sanctuary was set towards the west which is a peculiarity frequently seen in Pallava temples; almost all the temples of Mahâbalipuram and many of the Pallava temples at Kâñchipuram face the west.

The discovery of the temple of Paramêśvara at Kûram is important from two points of view :

1° It is interesting to identify the temple that was the object of the Kûram grant.

2° This temple is in ruins; however, what remains of it constitutes the most ancient monument in South India which is known to have been built of stones placed one above another.

§ VI.—In Chapter I of "*Pallava Antiquities*" we have spoken about the son of Paramêśvaravarman I., Narasiṁhavarman II. surnamed Râjasiṁha. He is perhaps the only Pallava king who had a long and peaceful reign. He does not seem to have done any thing else during his reign except loading the Śivite priests with favours and building the temples mentioned above, the Kailâsanâtha temple at Kâñchîpuram, the Shore temple at Mahâbalipuram and the Panamalai temple. To this list we may add the Airâvatêśvara temple at Kâñchîpuram. This temple with its rearing lions, the image of Sômâskanda and the prismatic liṅgam presents all the characteristics of the style of Râjasimha. Mr. A. Rea, relying upon its general aspect, has attributed this temple to the Pallavas. However, Epigraphy has as yet furnished no proof that will allow us to classify this temple definitively among the works of the reign of Râjasimha.

This temple whose Pallava origin is doubted has never been visited, however, by the officers of Epigraphical Department. When, in January 1917, I went to Mâmandûr, I stopped at Kâñchîpuram and visited all the temples there hoping to make some discovery.

The temple of Airâvatêśvara stands amidst a group of houses found opposite to the entrance of Kakhêśvara temple.

On examining this monument, I found all round the base of the temple some inscriptions which are very much damaged. One part is written in Tamil and the other in Grantha.

To the right of the entrance and at the base of the temple I found a fragment of an inscription and copied it as its importance cannot be questioned : the name नरसिंह Narasimha is written very clearly (vide Pl. III, C.).

§ VII.—Parmêśvaravarman II, son of Râjasimha, is probably the author of Vaikuṇtha Perumal temple at Kâñchîpuram.

The temple of Vîrattânêśvara at Tiruvâdi contains an inscription (No. 56 of 1903) belonging to the reign of Paramêśvara-Pôttaraiyar. In p. 72 of "*Pallava Antiquities*" Vol. I., I have spoken about the resemblance between the Vimâna of the Tiruvâdi temple and that of the Kailâsanâtha temple at Kâñchîpuram. Therefore, we must perhaps attribute the Śiva temple at Tiruvâdi to King Paramêśvaravarman II. However, this temple seems to have been repaired many times (we know, from inscription 35 of 1903, that it was done during the reign of Nṛipatuṅga).

The Tiruvâdi inscription is dated in the 3rd year of the reign of Paramêśvaravarman. It is probable that his reign was short.

CHAPTER V.

INTRODUCTION TO THE HISTORY OF THE DYNASTY OF NANDIVARMAN.

§ 1.—The Ganga-Pallava theory.

In 1887, there lived in India a gentleman who has rendered eminent service to the history of the Pallavas and whose name must not therefore be forgotten: It was Mr. J. Delafon, who was a Magistrate at Pondicherry. He discovered at Bâhûr (near Pondicherry) the plates of Nṛipatuṅga and at Kâśakûḍi the plates of Nandivarman Pallavamalla.

These two important discoveries are not due to chance; they are the happy result of the active and disinterested researches of a savant who studied the history and the languages of India for a long time.

Mr. Vinson, Professor in the School of Oriental Languages, Paris, has given the complete text, Sanskṛit and Tamil, of the Bâhûr plates, in an article that forms part of the memoirs published by the above School for the Congress of Orientalists held in 1905. However, the works that are published in French are generally ignored by the scholars of India.

So, the Bâhûr grant came to be known only by a short summary of it given by Mr. Hultzsch in his article No 23, page 180 in Vol. IV. of Epigraphia Indica.

The text was republished a few days ago, but without translation, in Part V, Vol. II of *S.I.I.*, p. 514.

This text is incomplete: it is the work of a Pandit who lived at Pondicherry at the time of Mr. Delafon, and in many places the transcription is defective.

I thought it necessary to give the readers of this book the translation of the Bâhûr plates. So, I requested M. R. Ry. T. A. Gopinatha Rao to translate for me the Sanskṛit portion of the text as published in Vol. II of *S.I.I.*, and he has been good enough to send me the following version of it:

THE BÂHÛR INSCRIPTION.

Text.

(Please retain the text as it appears in Part V, Vol. II. of *South Indian Inscriptions*, with Mr. Kṛishṇa Śâstri's footnotes also. In addition to these, please add the following):—

1. For निसृष्ट in l. 1 of verse 1, read निघृष्ट.
2. The words बन्दियुक्तान्तान् in l. 1 of verse 11, is an incorrect reading of the passage by the original transcriber, the Paṇḍit. As it is, the passage is not clear.
3. For खण्डानि in l. 2 of the same verse, read कण्ठानि.
4. For कलावान् समरे, I propose to read कलावसमरे, in the battle of Kalâva or Kalâpa, a place which requires identification.
5. For सराज्यश्रीः in l. 2 of verse 16, read सराज्यश्रि. The river Arichit is the same as the Ariśilâṟu. It is usual for the final *t* of Sańskṛit words being read in Tamiḻ countries as *l*. This custom is still retained in its entirety and often in a ridiculous manner in the Malabar country. For example, in almost all Tamiḻ inscriptions it will be found that the phrase *chandrâdityavat* written as *chandrâdityaval*. In Malayâḷam, words like *tasmât* is pronounced as *tasmâl*; *kêchit*, *kiñchit*, as *kêchil* and *kiñchil* respectively. On this analogy we may argue that the Tamiḻ name Ariśil or Arichil was Sańskṛitised into Arichit. It must be remembered that almost all the battles between the Pallavas and the allied armies of the Pâṇḍyas and the Chôḷas, were fought in the vicinity of Kumbhakôṇam, near which is also the river Ariśilâṟu.
6. For देववत् in l. 1 of verse 20, read देहवत्. It is only then the passage makes any sense.
7. For आथवा in l. 2 of verse 20, read अथंवा.
8. For द्विशांपतेः in l. 2 of verse 20, read द्विशांपतिः.
9. For प्रात्रयं in l. 1 of verse 21, read प्रामत्रयं.
10. For ०राकरत्वेन in l. 2 of verse 27, read रकरत्वेन; and
11. For धर्म्मस्य in l. 2 of verse 29, read धर्म्मस्स.

Translation.

Verse 1.—May Madhusûdana, whose lotus-feet are rubbed by the *kirîtas* of the *dêvas*, who is the cause of the destruction of the Râkshasas who are dreaded by all the worlds, who is eternal and whose eyes resemble the petals of the lotus, give you prosperity.

V. 2.—.........From his naval rose the lotus flower which is the origin of every (created) thing; from it came Brahmâ.

V. 3.—From the lord of the world, the four-faced (Brahmâ), was born Aṅgiras. From him, Bṛihaspati, the minister of Śakra (Indra), the destroyer of (the *asura*) Vala.

V. 4.—From him Saṁyu; from him was born Bharadvâja. From him the great archer Drôṇa, who was as powerful in battle as Indra.

V. 5.—(Then) came into existence from Drôṇa Aśvatthâman of great power who was well-versed in the use of all weapons and who was a (partial) incarnation of Pinâkin (Śiva).

V. 6.—From Aśvatthâma was born the king named Pallava. He protected every one, from the cultivators up to the kings, in the Navakhaṇḍa (the nine divisions of the earth ?).

V. 7.—In his lineage were born the host (of kings), Vimala, Koṅkaṇika etc., before whom the wives of the enemies bowed, whose commands were obeyed by other kings also, who were most dear (to their subjects ?) and who were ever attended by the sound '*jaya*' (be ye victorious.)

Vv. 8-9.—After Vimala and others, having ruled the earth which is girdled by the four oceans, by their prowess had gone to heaven in celestial chariots (*vimânas*), there lived the king Dantivarman, who was equal to Indra (in his power), who was an intense devotee of Muradvish (= Murâri, Vishṇu), who was powerful and who was worshipped by their crowns by (other) kings.

V. 10.—This sovereign, on account of his ruling the earth even in this Kaliyuga with justice and of his pouring gifts, shone like Indra.

V. 11.—(This verse is incorrect. It appears to convey the following idea in it. Nandivarman cut his enemies' heads which resembled parcels of food offered to their souls which were preparing to pay a visit to the house of Yama).

V. 12.—From Dantivarman was born the powerful Nandivarman, who, singly and unaided, took the earth in battle.

V. 13.—Just as Lakshmî was (the wife) of Muradvish (Vishṇu), the queen named Śaṅkhâ, who was born in the Râshṭrakûta family, was the wife of Nandivarman.

V. 14.—Śaṅkhâ, the queen of the king, who resembled the earth in forbearance, who was kind to the people like a mother, was resplendent as Lakshmî incarnate.

V. 15.—Nṛipatuṅgadêva who was esteemed for his high birth, who was lord of the three worlds, who was resplendent as the rising sun and who was victorious in the battle of Kalâva (?) was born of that queen who had intelligence, beauty, learning etc.

V. 16.—The army (of the Pallavas) which on a former occasion sustained defeat in the hands of the Pâṇḍya, was, by the grace of this king (i.e., by being led by him), able to burn down the hosts of the enemies together with the prosperity of their kingdoms, on the bank of the river Arichit.

V. 17.—This illustrious king named Nṛipatuṅga though he was young (in age) was not only famous in this, but also in the other worlds, as Râma was.[1]

V. 18.—Mârttâṇḍa of Vêśâli who was born in the race of Kuru and who was solicitous in protecting his subjects, was bound by obligation to this king (Nṛipatuṅga.)

Vv. 19-20.—He was great in the world like the moon ; in majesty etc., he resembled the ocean ; he was an asylum to the world (the people) inasmuch as he afforded protection (to it) like the sun. Therefore it is but right that there should be similarity between his body and name.[2] Or, he is certainly a king because it is quite patent at sight (?)

1. Just as Râma, even as a boy, had conquered Râkshasas for Visvâmitra and become famous in this world and was held as an object of praise even by gods, Nripatunga became famous as a boy-warrior and king even in the world of gods.

2. He is named Mârttânda (meaning the sun) ; he exerts his energy in protecting the country : in this act he resembles the sun which sustains life on the earth by its warmth and energy. So, Mârttânda of the Vêśâli family and of the race of Kuru is akin in name and action to the sun. Here the reading has been slightly altered ; instead of *dêvavat*, I am inclined to read *dêhavat* which makes sense.

Vv. 21-23.—He, who was increasing (the prosperity of) the Kuru race, having petitioned Nṛipatuṅga and duly obtained permission through the Secretary (âjñapti), granted to the *vidyâsthâna* the three villages, namely, Chêtupâkkam, Viḷâṅgâdirêphântam (*i.e.*, Viḷâṅgâttûr) and Iṛaippuṇaich-chêri situated in his province (Vêśâlippâḍi).

Vv. 24-29.—Just as Dûrjaṭi (Śiva) bore on one of his *jaṭas* (the river) Gaṅgâ who was descending with a large number of waves, similarly the river of learning consisting of fourteen *gunas* (or divisions of knowledge) was spreading round the abode of the residents of the Bâhu-village: because it is the abode of learned men, it is called a *vidyâsthâna*.

This king, having given them (the learned men of Bâhûr) by his *âjñapti* the villages to the extent marked by the circumambulation of an elephant, freed from all taxes and protected thereby, honored himself.

The minister of the king Śrî Tuṅgavarman, who has reverential awe for the commands (of the king), who is of a charitable disposition, who is held in regard by the lord of the three worlds (perhaps this refers to the king), who is famous like Bṛihaspati (the minister of the lord of the celestials Indra), exhorts the future kings to protect this charity (made by him).

V. 30.—Dâśaya, the servant of the *vidyâsthâna* of the resident of Bâhu and who is himself learned in the principles of the *śâstras*, wrote this eulogistic document.

[TAMIL PORTION, LEFT UNTRANSLATED.]

V. 31.—"If equal merit accrues to both the giver of a charity and its protector ,then do you protect it."—so saying, the king Nṛipatuṅgavarman, by bowing lowly his head which bears on it the feet of Mukuṇda (Vishṇu), exhorts future kings.

V. 32.—The goldsmith Nṛipatuṅga, who was an ornament to the family of Uditôdita, who was well-versed in all *śâstras* and who was an hereditary servant of the Pallavas wrote this document.

The Bâhûr plates were discovered at a time when the Epigraphy of South India was yet unborn. The dynasty: Ḍanti-

Nandi-Nṛipatuṅga, was quite new. No sooner had a few stone inscriptions been copied than Mr. Hultzsch tried to reconcile the new records with that of Bâhûr.

Owing to an unlucky chance, there was, among the discoveries that were made first, the Kîḻ-Muttugûr inscription which Mr. Hultzsch has published with the following remark (*Ep. Ind.*, Vol. IV, p. 177):

« The inscription is dated in the eighteenth year of the reign » of the king, the Victorious Narasiṁhavarman. The same name » occurs among the Pallava kings of Kâñchî. But the two centre » figures of the bas-relief below the inscription make it impossible » to attribute this record to the Pallava Dynasty, whose crest was » a bull and whose banner bore a club. The elephant appears at » the top of three stone inscriptions of the Western Gaṅga » dynasty which have been published by Mr. Kikel, and the goose » (haṁsa) is said to have been the device on the banner of the » mythical Gaṅga king Koṅkaṇi.»

In editing the two inscriptions of Nṛipatuṅga found at Ambûr (*Ep. Ind.*, Vol. IV, p. 180), Mr. Hultzsch has said:

« Besides, the Bâhûr plates mention among Nṛipatuṅga- » varman's remote ancestors Koṅkaṇika. This name seems to be » a reminiscence of Koṅkaṇi, who is believed to have been the » ancestor of the Western Gaṅgas.»

And again (*Ep. Ind.*, Vol. IV, p. 182):

« The Kîḻ-Muttugûr inscription of the latter (Narasiṁha- » varman) bears, however, the emblems of the W. Gaṅga kings » and its alphabet is more archaic than that of the two Âmbûr » inscriptions of Nṛipatuṅga. If it is kept in mind that the » Bâhûr plates represent the latter [Nṛipatuṅga] as a descendant » not only of Pallava, but also of Koṅkaṇi, the ancestor of the » Western Gaṅga kings, we are driven to the conclusion that the » old dynasty of the Pallavas of Kâñchî came to an end with » Nandivarman, the opponent of the Western Châlukya king » Vikramâditya II: that Narasiṁhavarman, a Pallava by name, » but Western Gaṅga by descent, succeeded them; that two of » his successors, Dantivarman and Nandivarman, were the con- » temporaries of the Râshtrakûta kings Gôvinda III. and Amôgha- » varsha I; and that Nandivarman's son, Nṛipatuṅgavarman or » Nṛipatuṅga - Vikramavarman, who ruled over North Arcot,

» Tanjore and Trichinopoly, discarded the emblems of the Western » Gaṅgas and adopted those of the Pallavas.»

The Gaṅga-Pallava theory that has been imagined by Mr. Hultzsch is very simple; it can be summarised in a few words:

Nṛipatuṅga is not a descendant of Naṅdivarman Pallavamalla; he is not a Pallava; he has usurped this title; the name Koṅkaṇika, found in the genealogy given in the Bâhûr plates, proves that he is a descendant, not of Nandivarman Pallavamalla, but of certain chiefs of Western Gaṅga origin.

The whole of the Gaṅga-Pallava theory is, therefore, based on the word Koṅkaṇika. Was this name quite enough to justify the creation of a new dynasty?

Mr. Hultzsch has made a supposition, a hypothesis, based on a very weak argument, which cannot be admitted unless confirmed by other discoveries; and until this is done, it must remain what it really is, *viz.*, a simple conjecture.

The inscriptions dated during the reigns of kings like Dantivarman (*e.g.*, inscription No. 80 of 1898), Nandivarman (*e.g.*, No. 72 of 1898), Nṛipatuṅga (*e.g.*, No. 81 of 1898), ought to be classed among the Pallava inscriptions up to the time when the Gaṅga origin of Nṛipatuṅga and his ancestors is proved in an irrefutable manner.

Mr. Hultzsch has not had the discretion to do so. In his report on Epigraphy for 1897 (*G. O.*, Nos. 1093-1096, 29th Aug. 1898) inscription No. 304 of 1897 of Vijaya-Nandivikramavarman —17th year—is classed under the head of "Gaṅga-Pallava".

So, even when there is not sufficient evidence to confirm this imprudent theory, it has received official sanction.

The Gaṅga-Pallava dynasty was ranked with the great Pallava, Chôḷa and Pâṇḍya dynasties.

For that, and that alone, Mr. Hultzsch deserved to be reproached.

He had every right to imagine that Nṛipatuṅga was of Gaṅga origin and write in the "Epigraphia Indica" the sentences we have quoted.

But he had no right to put during 6 years (from 1897 to 1904) a great number of inscriptions in the Gaṅga-Pallava category, as if the existence of this dynasty had been completely established.

First of all, it must be proved:

1° that Nṛipatuṅga was actually descended from a king named Koṅkaṇika;

2° that the above Koṅkaṇika was no other than the Gaṅga king Koṅkaṇi;

3° that Nṛipatuṅga was not also a descendant of Nandivarman Pallavamalla.

M. Hultzsch seems to have thought such proofs useless: similarity of names, vague suppositions, unfounded identifications based on imaginary genealogies, all these have formed a respectable whole for enabling him to consider the Gaṅga origin of Nṛipatuṅga as something conclusively proved.

It was not necessary, since then, to prove the Gaṅga-Pallava theory; the hypothesis of Mr. Hultzsch need not be confirmed by other discoveries: *it was true by supposition.*

So, we have to lay much stress on the fact that "*the Ganga-Pallava theory has been admitted without any demonstration.*"

We have so far examined "The Hultzsch theory." We shall now enter into the second stage and examine what we may call "The Venkayya theory."

In editing the inscription of Dantivarman found at Triplicane, V. Venkayya has written (*Ep. Ind.* Vol. VIII, No. 29, p. 291):

« The inscription.........is dated during the reign of King » Dantivarma-Mahârâja, who was "the ornament of the Pallava » family" and belonged to the Bhâradvâja-gôtra. There is thus no » doubt that he belonged to the Pallava dynasty.»

In his report on Epigraphy for 1905-06 (*G. O.* No. 492, 2nd July, 1906) V. Venkayya mentions inscription No. 541 of 1905 dated during the « reign of Dantivarman of the Pallavatilaka » family, which sprang from the Bhâradvâja-gôtra »: « From other » inscriptions we know that the queen of a certain Nandippôtta- » raiyaṉ of the Pallavatilaka family lived as late as the time of » the Gaṅga-Pallava king Nṛipatuṅga and the reign of the Chôḷa » king Râja Kêsarivarman (Annual Report for 1900-01, paragraph » 10). Consequently, the original Pallavas of Conjeeveram seem » to have continued in some form or other long after the defeat of » Nandivarman Pallavamalla by the Western Chalukya Vikra- » mâditya II., when they apparently ceased to be the dominant » power in Southern India. The political relationship of the » Pallavas to the Gaṅga-Pallavas, who gradually took their place, » is not known.»

So V. Venkayya lays down a principle: « When, in an inscription, a king is said to belong to the Pallava dynasty—there is no doubt that he belonged to the Pallava dynasty.»

Applying this principle, V. Venkayya affirms that kings like Dantivarman of Triplicane and Tiruveḷḷaṛai and Nandippôttaraiyaṉ "of Pallavatilaka family" are really Pallavas, and that, therefore, the Pallava dynasty has continued to exist after the death of Nandivarman Pallavamalla.

If V. Venkayya had been logical, he would have carried his conclusions further. In the Bâhûr plates, it is distinctly stated that Danti, his son Nandi and his grandson Nṛipatuṅga are all descended from the Pallavas and belong to the Bhâradvâja-gôtra.

If here V. Venkayya had applied the principle laid down by him, he would have said of Nṛipatuṅga: « There is thus no doubt that he belonged to the Pallava dynasty.»

But V. Venkayya could not agree to it. The name Koṅkaṇika found in the genealogy given in the Bâhûr plates has been considered by Mr. Hultzsch as positive proof of the Gaṅga origin of Nṛipatuṅga. It is not therefore possible to doubt it. The descendants of Nandivarman Pallavamalla could not therefore be identified with the ancestors of Nṛipatunga; there were therefore two different dynasties reigning at the same time.

Then, V. Venkayya created a new theory founded on the following principles:

1° The Pallava dynasty existed after Nandivarman Pallavamalla. Dantivarman of Triplicane and Nandippôttaraiyaṉ are their representatives. They differ from the "Gaṅga-Pallavas" by their epithets "Pôttaraiyaṉ," "pôtavarman" [pôta in Saṅskrit and pôttu in Tamil mean 'the sprout (of a plant)' and are thus synonymous with pallava, "a sprout"— *S.I.I.*, Vol. II, p. 341]. "Pallava-kula-tilaka": "The title Pallava-Kulatilaka of the former (Dantivarman) which occurs in the Triplicane inscription might have furnished the family name Pallavatilakakula of his successors, which must have been invented in order to distinguish them from the rising Gaṅga-Pallavas (*G. O.* No. 492— 2nd July 1906)."

2° At the same time there existed a dynasty of chiefs of Gaṅga origin, such as Narasiṁhavarman of Kîḻ-Muttugûr, Danti, Nandi and Nṛipatuṅga of Bâhûr. These chiefs have succeeded by degrees in supplanting the true Pallavas. They are distinguished by the prefix "Vijaya" or the suffix "Vikramavarman".

When V. Venkayya enunciated this theory, there was but one person who strongly protested against it.

In an article published in April 1907 in the "*Christian College Magazine*" under the heading "The Pallavas and the Gaṅga-Pallavas"—M. R. Ry. T. A. Gopinatha Rao, Superintendent of Archæology, Travancore State, Trevandram, has enunciated the following propositions:

1° The Gaṅga origin of Nṛipatuṅga which « has been treated » as a sort of axiomatic truth by later epigraphists (p. 1) » is a wrong supposition.

2° There existed but one dynasty, that of the Pallavas; the descendants of Nandivarman Pallavamalla must be identified with the ancestors of Nṛipatuṅga.

3° Dantivarman, the grand-father of Nṛipatuṅga is the son of Nandivarman Pallavamalla.

The last hypothesis is very remarkable. M. R. Ry. T. A. Gopinatha Rao was the first to affirm that Pallavamalla was the father of Dantivarman. So, the genealogy of the Pallavas stands thus:

Nandivarman Pallavamalla
|
Dantivarman
|
Nandivarman
|
Nṛipatuṅga

However, no one cared for what was said by M. R. Ry. Gôpinâtha Rao. V. Venkayya continued to maintain his own opinion, and the public, relying on the authority of the Government Epigraphist, continued to believe in Gaṅga-Pallavas.

This was in 1907. Ten years have rolled on since and new discoveries have only confirmed in a striking manner the theory of M.R.Ry. T.A. Gopinatha Rao.

1° Although we possess a large number of documents, we have not as yet found any proof of Nṛipatuṅga being related to Narasiṁhavarman of Kiḷ-Muttugûr or to the Gaṅgas.

2° In none of the numerous known inscriptions has it been possible to find the least trace of any internal struggle enabling us to believe that the Ganga-Pallavas supplanted the descendants of Nandivarman Pallavamalla. There has been no civil war, no revolution, no dissension in the Pallava Kingdom.

3°. The inscriptions of the Pallavas and the so-called Ganga-Pallavas are found scattered all over the country, and it must be admitted that these two different dynasties reigned over the same country at the same time:

« There would be an insuperable difficulty in locating these » two contemporary dynasties in proper geographical regions. » (The Pallavas and the Ganga-Pallavas—p. 8) ».

4° It has been proved that Nṛipatuṅga had the name that marks his Pallava origin : « The ending "pôttaraiyar" which is » applied to [Nṛipatuṅgappôttaraiyar of the Vaḷuvûr inscription » No. 68 of 1908] without the characteristic prefix Kô-viśaiya, » makes it suspicious if we could include his name among the » Gaṅga-Pallavas (*G.O.* No 538, 28th July 1909).»

Moreover, the discovery of the Vêlûrpâḷaiyam plates has shown (*G.O.* No. 832, 28th July 1911) that the descendants of Nandivarman Pallavamalla had the prefix Kô-vijaya and the suffix Vikramavarman added to their names.

The same Vêlûrpâḷaiyam plates have proved the following genealogy in an incontestable manner:

Nandivarman-Pallavamalla
|
Dantivarman
|
Kô-vijaya-Nandivikramavarman.

If we bear in mind, that, in 1907, i.e., 4 years before the discovery of these plates, M. R. Ry. T. A. Gopinatha Rao had affirmed that Dantivarman was the son of Nandivarman Pallavamalla, we shall see the barrenness of the Gaṅga-Pallava theory and the fecundity of the theory propounded by M. R. Ry. Gopinatha Rao.

And still, up to this time, it has been possible to doubt it, as the conclusive argument in favour of Mr. T. A. Gopinatha Rao's theory has not been found. What was, in fact, the origin and basis of the Gaṅga-Pallava theory? It was the name Koṅkaṇika in the genealogy given in the Bâhûr plates.

Mr. Hultzsch said, and V. Venkayya repeated with him, « Nṛipatuṅga is not a Pallava; he is a Gaṅga because he is » descended from Koṅkaṇika». That was the only reason. M. R. Ry.

T. A. Gopinatha Rao said that that reason was good for nothing; he gathered proofs to try to demolish the Gaṅga-Pallava theory, but its supporters retorted, « Nṛipatuṅga is not a Pallava; he is descended from Koṅkaṇika.»

In publishing the Vêlûrpâḷaiyam plates in Part V of Vol. II of *S. I. I.* that appeared only a few days ago (Madras, 1917), M. R. Ry. H. Krishna Sastri says of the theory of M. R. Ry. T. A. Gopinatha Rao that it « connects the names in the Bâhûr » plates with those of the Vêlûrpâḷaiyam plates, and suggests » that Vijaya Nṛipatuṅgavarman of the former was apparently » the son of Nandivarman III of the latter » (*S. I. I.*, Vol. II, Part V, No. 98, p. 505).

Rao Sahib H. Krishna Sastri then says distinctively: « Against this, the **only** objection is the ancestry which, in the » one case includes the clear Western Gaṅga name (or surname) » Koṅkaṇika, while in the other it does not.»

To-day (June 1917) this objection does not exist any more: the deciphering of the Vâyalûr inscription has cleared all doubt.

We have said in Chapter II of this book that the Vâyalûr inscription gives us a complete genealogy of the ancestors of Narasiṁhavarman II (Râjasiṁha).

After Pallava, Aśôka, Harigupta, Âryavarman and some others, we have the following series: Kâḷinda, Byâmalla, [E]ka-malla, Vimala, Koṅkaṇika, Kâḷabhartṛi, Chûtapallava, Vîrakûrcha.

We have reproduced in Pl. II the estampage of this part of the inscription.

We have said that the presence of names of Western Gaṅga origin, such as, Âryavarman and Koṅkaṇika, in a genealogy of the Pallavas engraved on stone in the VII century, shows the political relations and perhaps also the bonds of affinity that existed between the Western Gaṅgas and the Pallavas in the VI century of the Christian era. The Peṇugoṇḍa plates (*G.O.*, No. 920, 4th Aug. 1914, Part II, No. 4, p. 86) confirm this hypothesis, as they say that the grandson of Koṅkaṇivarman who was called Âryavarman was installed on the throne by the Pallava king Siṁhavarman and that perhaps he married the daughter of this Pallava king since we see that his son was named Siṁhavarman. The son of Siṁhavarman, alias Madhava II, was Koṅkaṇivarman II alias Avinîta [Śringêri plates—Mysore Archœological Report for 1916, p. 33.]

Genealogy of the W. Gangas.

Approximate dates:

A. D.

420 Koṅkaṇivarman (I).

450 Mâdhava (I).

480 Âryavarman (installed on the throne by Siṁhavarman, a Pallava king).

510 Siṁhavarman alias Mâdhava (II) (installed by Skandavarman Pallava). (Penugoṇḍa plates).

540 Koṅkaṇivarman (II) alias Aviṇîta
[Śringêri plates—Mysore Report for 1916, p. 33.]
[E.C. 10, Mâlûr 72.]

580 Druvinîta
(Muḷbâgal plates— Mysore Report for 1916, p. 44.)
[Gummareḍḍipura plates— Mysore Report for 1912 dated the 40th year.]

We have proved with the help of the Vâyalûr inscription that the names Vimala and Koṅkaṇika existed in the Pallava genealogy from the VII century.

The presence of these names in the Bâhûr genealogy goes only to confirm the purely Pallava origin of Nṛipatuṅga.

Thus then, from the moment that the Vâyalûr inscription was deciphered, the Gaṅga-Pallavas ceased to exist; full light has been thrown on the dynasty of Nṛipatuṅga; the truth is seen to be clear and simple, and it can be summed up in the following words: M. R. Ry. T. A. Gopinatha Rao was right in affirming that—

1° in the VIII and the IX centuries there existed but one dynasty, that of the Pallavas;

2° the Vêlûrpâḷaiyam plates coupled with those of Bâhûr give us the following genealogy:

Nandivarman (Pallavamalla).

Dantivarman

Nandivarman (donor of the Vêlûrpâḷaiyam plates).

Nṛipatuṅga (donor of the Bâhûr plates).

§ 2. Chronology.

Let us first determine the duration of each reign. This question presents no difficulties in regard to Dantivarman and Nṛipatuṅga.

The inscription (No. 262 of 1904) at Tiruchchâṉûr is dated in the 51st year of Dantivarman. That implies a long reign and we shall admit that Dantivarman reigned little more than 51 years.

It is certain that Nṛipatuṅga reigned 26 years, for the inscriptions of this king, which are very numerous, do not go beyond the 26th year.

The question is not so simple in the case of the two other kings. We know, as a matter of fact, that both of them bear the name of Nandivarman.

How to distinguish the one Nandi from the other? and how long did each of them reign?

I hold a very definite opinion on this subject. I shall now proceed to prove my proposition, which is quite different from what has been imagined till now. I am the first to enunciate it and I strongly affirm it as I am quite convinced of it.

Nandivarman Pallavamalla reigned 62 years. His grandson reigned for about 24 years.

My demonstration is based on the Taṇḍantôṭṭam plates.

In the 58th year of his reign, a king Vijaya-Nandivikramavarman has made this grant (*S.I.I.*, Vol. II, Part V, No. 99, p. 517).

These plates have been, till now, attributed to the king that granted the Vêlûrpaḷaiyam plates, viz., to the son of Danti. My opinion is quite the reverse.

The donor of the Taṇḍantôṭṭam plates is Nandivarman Pallavamalla. Here are my reasons for thinking so:

1° *From the palæographic point of view:*

(*a*) If the donor of the Taṇḍantôṭṭam plates were the same as the donor of the Vêlûrpâḷaiyam plates, as the first is dated in the 58th year and the second in the 6th year, the alphabet of the Vêlûrpâḷaiyam plates must be more archaic: but it is just the reverse: *The alphabet of the Taṇḍantôṭṭam plates is more archaic than that of the Vêlûrpâḷaiyam plates.*

In the Sanskṛit portion of the Taṇḍantôṭṭam plates, the letters, â, kha, ga, da, dha, na, ya, va, śa, sa, ha, nâ, mu, tê, to, show signs of archaism, when compared with the corresponding letters in the Vêlûrpâḷaiyam plates.

It is the same case with the Tamil letters: ṅa, ta, na, ya, la, tâ, nâ, yî, mû, lai, ko, to.

It must therefore be admitted that the Nandi of the Taṇḍantôttam plates was a predecessor of the Nandi of the Vêlûrpâḷaiyam plates.

(*b*) If, instead of examining the letters separately, we observe the general aspect of the writing, we shall find that the Taṇḍantôttam plates remind us of the Kâśâkuḍi plates, whereas the Vêlûrpâḷaiyam plates resemble those of Hastimalla found at Udayendiram. For example, vertical lines predominate in the Taṇḍantôttam plates; besides that, the secondary *i* is almost circular; on the contrary, the vertical lines are scarcely visible in the Vêlûrpâḷaiyam plates and the secondary *i* is semi-circular.

(*c*) If, instead of comparing the plates, we view them individually, we are led to the following considerations:

If we suppose that the Taṇḍantôttam plates were dated in the 58th year of the reign of the son of Danti, they would evidently belong to the end of the IX century.

We know, in fact, that Danti was vanquished about 804 A.D. by Govinda III (*G. O.* No. 919, 29th July 1912, p. 59, Part II, No. 7). Granting that this date falls at the end of Danti's reign and that he died in 805, the 58th year of the reign of his son would be 805 + 58 = 863.

So, if we admit that the Taṇḍantôttam plates are dated in the reign of Nandi, son of Danti, they would be dated 863 or some years after, i.e., at the end of the IX century. There would then be a difference of 50 years between them and the plates of Bâṇâ King Hastimalla (*S.I.I.*, Vol. II, Part III, plate facing p. 385.)

Any one who has a look at the Taṇḍantôttam plates (*S.I.I.*, Vol. II, Plate XVIII) will, I think, admit that *the alphabet of the Tandantôttam plates is much too archaic to be attributed to the second half of the IX Century (about 870)*.

I think that these plates are one century older and belong to the second half of the VIII century (about 775).

2° A reign of more than half a century is rare in history; and there is no room to doubt that the inscription (No. 10 of 1895) at Pañchapâṇḍavamalai dated in the 50th year of the reign of

Nandippôttaraśar belongs to the same reign as the Taṇḍantôṭṭam plates which are dated in the 58th year of the reign of Nandi."

If then this king was the son of Danti, it must be admitted that the Pañchapâṇḍavamalai inscription belongs to the second half of the IX Century. I think it is absolutely impossible to do so. The alphabet of this inscription is archaic : for example, in the latter half of the IX century, the letter *va* began with a curve ; in the Pañchapâṇḍavamalai inscription there is no curve (Vide Plate : *Ep. Ind.*, Vol IV).

3° From the genealogical point of view, we know that there was only one Pallava prince who was called Hiraṇyavarman. The inscription (No. 37 of 1888) on the wall of the southern verandah in the Vaikuṇtha-Perumâl temple at Kâñchîpuram leads us to believe, and the Kâśâkuḍi plates say very clearly, that this prince was the father of Nandivarman Pallavamalla.

And the Taṇḍantôttam plates say distinctly that Nandivarman, the donor, is the son of Hiraṇyavarman.

There is therefore no room for any doubt. Nandivarman, son of Hiraṇyavarman, who, in the 58th year of his reign, made the Taṇḍantôttam grant is no other than Nandivarman Pallavamalla.

4° When Nandivarman Pallavamalla granted, by the Kâśâkuḍi plates, the village of Koḍukoḷḷi, it received the new name of Êkadhîramaṅgalam ; from this we may conclude that Pallavamalla was surnamed Êkadhîra.

And Nandi, the donor of the Taṇḍantôttam plates, is designated in verse 4 of these plates by the surname Êkadhîra.

M. R. Ry. H. Krishna Sastri says : " Dantivarman mentioned in No. 88 of Appendix C from Tiruveḷḷaṟai is reported to have belonged to the Brahma, kshatra family and to have been entitled Pallava-Mahârâja. Evidently, the double name Dantinandivarman has to be understood in the sense of Nandivarman, son of Dantivarman......The title Pallava-Mahârâja borne by him, may point to the fact that he was a Pallava king, and perhaps identical with Nandippôttaraiyar of the Tiruchcheṉṉambûṇḍi inscription, (No. 283 of 1901), " who was victorious at Teḷḷâṟu."

This hypothesis is confirmed by the fact that the inscriptions of the victor of Teḷḷâṟu are written in an alphabet which is not archaic enough to be attributed to the epoch of Nandivarman Pallavamalla.

Besides, the Nandikkalambagam gives a description of the victor of Teḷḷâṛu which cannot apply to Nandivarman Pallavamalla.

And M. R. Ry. T. A. Gopinatha Rao, relying upon the fact that a certain Kâḍuvetti-Tamiḻappêraraiyan was a contemporary of both the victor of Teḷḷâṛu and Nṛipatuṅga, concluded, as early as 1907 (Madras Christian College Magazine April 1907, page 8), that the former (Nandi) was the father of the latter (Nṛipatunga).

It is therefore probable that the Victor of Teḷḷâṛu was the son of Dantivarman and the father of Nṛipatuṅga.

As, on the other hand, we do not know of any inscription of this king dated after the 22nd year of his reign, we may conclude:

1° Nandivarman Pallavamalla reigned 62 years.

2° Nandivarman Teḷḷâṛreṛinda reigned only a little more than 22 years.

As I am convinced that the Gudimallam inscription (No. 229 of 1903) is dated in the 23rd year of the reign of this latter king, [the alphabet of this inscription mostly resembles that of the inscription No. 228 of 1903 dated during the reign of Nṛipatuṅga] I think we can give him a reign of about 24 years.

The inscription of Tiruvallam (No. 76 of 1889) being dated in the 62nd year of the reign of Nandi, we come to the conclusion that Nandivarman Pallavamalla reigned 62 years.

We have now determined the duration of the reigns:

Nandi-Ekadhîra-Pallavamalla : 62 years.
Dantivarman : 51 years.
Nandi-Teḷḷâṛreṛinda : 24 years.
Nṛipatuṅga : 26 years.

It would be desirable to know approximately when these kings reigned.

We can at once say for certain that they have reigned after the VII and before the IX Century.

1° *Pallavamalla began to reign after the VII century.*

In the preceding chapter, we have established, in an irrefutable manner, the fact that Paramêśvaravarman I. repulsed the Châlukyas in A. D. 674. Here we have a correct date. And between this and the accession of Nandivarman Pallavamalla there have passed away:

(*a*) the end of the reign of Paramêśvaravarman I;

(*b*) the whole of the reign of Narasiṁhavarman II. (Râjasiṁha), which was probably long enough;

(*c*) the reign of Paramêśvaravarman II., which was probably short.

I think these events must have taken 40 years, and so I conclude that it is unlikely that Nandivarman Pallavamalla began to reign before 716 or 717.

2° *Nripatunga's reign came to an end before 900.*

(*a*) Inscription No. 28 of 1903 is dated in the 24th year of the reign of Nṛipatuṅga, during the reign of his feudatory, the Bâṇa king Vâṇavijjâdhara; and the inscription No. 223 of 1903 is dated during the reign of the son of the Bâṇa king and in the Śaka year 820, *i.e.* 898 A.D. We must therefore conclude that the 24th year of Nṛipatuṅga's reign is anterior to 898 and that the 26th and last year is before 900.

(*b*) Inscription No. 735 of 1905 at Grâmam assures us that the Chôḷa king Parântaka I. began his reign in the first half of 907. (*G.O.* No. 492, 2nd July 1906, p. 68).

The year 906 is therefore the last year of the reign of his father Âditya I. But the Tirukkaḻukkuṇṛam (*Ep. Ind.*, Vol. III., p. 277) and the Brahmadeśam (No. 230 of 1915) inscriptions are dated in the 27th year of a king called Râjakêsarivarman, who must unquestionably be Âditya I., for he is the only king named Râjakêsari who was able to reign so long before Râja-râja. It is thus certain that Âditya I. ascended the throne about 880.

This king, who was surnamed Toṇḍaimâṇâṟṟûr-Tuñjiṇa-Uḍaiyâr gave his donations, in the North Arcot District, in the 21st and the 22nd years of his reign (*G.O.* No. 503, 27th June 1907, p. 71, part II, No. 29.) There is no doubt that this king was Âditya I, for an error that had been made in the donation was rectified during the reign of his son Parântaka I.

It is thus established that the Pallava empire was conquered by Âditya I. before the 21st year of his reign, *i.e.*, before 900 A.D.

So, it is between 717 and 900 that we must put the four reigns: Nandi, 62 years; Danti, 51 years; Nandi, 24 years; Nṛipatuṅga, 26 years.

The length of these four reigns put together g.ves a period of 62+51+24+26=163 years, and from 715 to 900 there are 185 years.

I therefore consider the following result as something certain:

The coronation of Nandivarman Pallavamalla took place between 717 & 737.

do.	Dantivarman	do.	779 & 799.
do.	Nandi of Teḷḷâṛu	do.	830 & 850.
do.	Nṛipatuṅga	do.	854 & 874.

These figures are confirmed by the following two facts which we shall prove later on:

1° Nandivarman Pallavamalla was vanquished by the Châlukyas about 741.

2° Dantivarman was vanquished by the Râshṭrakûṭas about 803.

If we now take the average of the two dates in which these kings might possibly have been crowned, we find that:

Nandivarman Pallavamalla	was crowned in	cir. A.D.	727.
Dantivarman	do.	do.	789.
Nandi of Teḷḷâṛu	do.	do.	840.
Nṛipatuṅga	do.	do.	864.

These figures may be considered to be approximately correct, allowing for an error of 10 years, more or less. This result must be considered sufficient.

I believe, however, that these 10 years can be taken away from the figures I have given above. I give below the reasons that have led me to this conclusion:

1° The Ambûr inscriptions (Nos. 7 and 8 of 1896—Vide also *Ep. Ind.*, Vol. IV, pp. 182 & 183) which are dated in the 26th and last year of the reign of Nṛipatuṅga mention Pirudi-Gaṅgaraiyar as a contemporary of this king.

It is probable that this Pirudi-Gaṅgaraiyar is no other than Pṛithvîpati I. whose last known date is 879. If we admit that the 26th year of Nṛipatuṅga almost coincides with this epoch, we must admit that Nṛipatuṅga ascended the throne about 854, which is 10 years before the approximate date we have given to it.

2° Inscription No. 222 of 1911, dated in the second year of Râjakêsarivarman and found at Tirunâgêśvaram in the Tanjore district, has been attributed by M. R. Ry. H. Krishna Sastri to Âditya I.

Inscriptions Nos. 101, 104, 105, 127, 130 and 133 of 1914 have been admitted by Diwan Bahadur L. D. Swamikannu Pillai (*G.O.* No. 1260, 25th Aug. 1915, p. 72, Appendix F.) to be "earlier than 907 A.D." and attributed by M. R. Ry. H. Krishna Sastri to Âditya I. (*Part II*, No. 20, p. 96, of the same Report).

These inscriptions are dated in the 5th, 6th, and 7th years of his reign and are engraved in the temple at Tiruveṟumbur in the Trichinopoly district.

If, then, we admit that these inscriptions are dated during the reign of Âditya I., we must also admit that this king was from the very beginning of his reign, *i.e.*, in 882 (2nd year of his reign) and 885 (5th year of his reign) the supreme lord of the districts of Tanjore and Trichinopoly.

But we must also bear in mind that Nṛipatuṅga reigned at Kaṇḍiyûr, near Tanjore, in the 21st year of his reign (insc. No. 17 of 1895) and that in the 22nd year he reigned at Lâlguḍi (insc. No. 83 of 1892) and at Kôvilaḍi (insc. Nos. 300 and 301 of 1901) which are situated not far from Tiruveṟumbur near Trichinopoly.

Thus then, the districts of Tanjore and Trichinopoly formed the kingdom of Nṛipatuṅga at the end of his reign and of Âditya at the beginning of the reign of the latter.

My impression is that Âḍitya I. began to reign after the death of Nṛipatuṅga who ceased to reign about 880. He should therefore have ascended the throne in 854, *i.e.*, 10 years before the approximate date (864) we have fixed for it.

3° The Udayendiram and the Kâśâkuḍi plates which are dated in the 21st and the 22nd year respectively of the reign of Nandivarman Pallavamalla do not mention the Châlukyan invasion that took place about 741. We may therefore conclude that those years of that king's reign are anterior to this event, and that Nandivarman Pallavamalla began to reign before 719-720.

For these reasons, I think that the approximate dates we have settled must be reduced by 10 years and I therefore fix the following chronology:

Nandivarman-Pallavamalla:	from 717 to 779	A.D.
Dantivarman:	„ 779 to 830	„
Nandi of Teḷḷâṟu:	„ 830 to 854	„
Nṛipatuṅga:	„ 854 to 880	„

§ 3. The History of the Pâṇḍyas.

We have said that, about 741, during the reign of Nandivarman Pallavamalla, there was a Châlukyan invasion and that about 803, king Dantivarman became a tributary of the Râshṭrakûṭas.

Apart from these two events, I believe that most of the wars that the Pallavas had to wage were against the Pâṇḍyas; so, in writing the history of the Pallavas we must speak of the Pâṇḍyas.

We shall begin the history of the Pâṇḍyas by putting the genealogy of Vêḷvikuḍi by the side of that of the two Śiṉṉamaṉûr as shown below:

Vêḷvikuḍi grant [Report for 1908]		Sinnamanur plates
1) Kaḍungôn		
2) Mâṟavarman Avaniśuḷâmaṇi		
3) Śeḻiyaṉ Śêndaṉ	— 1) Jayantavarman	Smaller Śiṉṉamaṉûr [Report for 1907]
4) Arikêsarin Mâṟavarman	— 2) Arikêsarin Mâṟavarman	Smaller Śiṉṉamaṉûr [Report for 1907]
5) Kôchchaḍaiyaṉ		
6) Ter Mâran Râjasiṁha	— 1) Arikêsarin Parâṅkuśaṉ	Bigger Śiṉṉamaṉûr plates. [Report for 1907]
7) Jaṭila Parantâka	— 2) Jaṭila	Bigger Śiṉṉamaṉûr plates. [Report for 1907]
	3) Râjasiṁha	Bigger Śiṉṉamaṉûr plates. [Report for 1907]
	4) Varaguṇa	Bigger Śiṉṉamaṉûr plates. [Report for 1907]
	5) Mâra, Êkavîra Srîvallabha Parachakrakôlâhala	Bigger Śiṉṉamaṉûr plates. [Report for 1907]

The first king that seems to be a little known to fame is No. 4 Arikêsarin Mâṟavarman.

The Vêḷvikuḍi plates say: « He overcame the ocean-like » army of Vilvêli at the battle of Nelvêli and conquered the army » of the king of Kêraḷa »; and the Tiruttoṇḍattogai of Sundaramûrti Nâyaṉâr (verse 8) mentions a king named "Neḍumâṟan, who was victorious in the battle of Nelvêli," who was first a Jain, was afterwards converted to Śivism by Tiruñâṉasambandar and became one of the 63 devotees. If therefore this saintly king is identified with No. 4 Mâṟavarman, he will be the contemporary of Sambandar.

The latter was a contemporary (Periyapuranam—p. 318) of Śiṟuttoṇḍa - Nâyaṉar who conquered Vâtâpi with Narasiṁhavarman I. King No. 4, Mâṟavarman would therefore have lived about 650.

His son, No. 5 Kôchchaḍaiyan would have lived about 675.

The Vêḷvikuḍi plates say of him: « He destroyed at Marudûr » the ocean-like army and at the great city of Maṅgalapuram » the Mahâratha was overcome and destroyed.» This victory at Marudûr, this ocean of enemies, this "Mahâratha", what are all these?

We have said just now that Kôchchaḍaiyan lived probably about 675. Strange coincidence! It is precisely in 674 that Vikramâditya I. was encamped at Uragapuram, *i.e.*, at Trichinopoly. And the Kêndûr plates (*Ep. Ind.* Vol. IX, No 29, p. 205) say that Vikramâditya I. fought with the Pâṇḍyas; we have also supposed that the Pâṇḍya king was one of the three confederates who gained the victory at Peruvaḷanallûr. The "Mahâratha" will then be the Châlukyan king.

The son of Kôchchaḍaiyan was Râjasiṁha. Here we find a new coincidence: we have supposed that Kôchchaḍaiyan and Paramêśvaravarman I. were friends allied together against Vikramâditya. The son of Kôchchaḍaiyan and the son of Paramêśvaravarman I. both bore the same name of Râjasiṁha. This can be explained by supposing that the Pallava prince Râjasiṁha (who was a lion to his enemies, probably the Châlukyas) fought under the orders of his father, Paramêśvaravarman I., on the side of Kôchchaḍaiyan; Kôchchaḍaiyan married the daughter of Râjasiṁha and the son of the Pâṇḍya king was given the name of his grandfather, the Pallava king.

There again we shall find a new coincidence:

The Udayendiram plates (*S.I.I.* Vol. II, part III, p. 376.) say that Nandivarman Pallavamalla faced a great danger. He was attacked by the Pallava prince Chitramâya and other princes among whom was the Pâṇḍya king who fought the battle of Maṇṇaikuḍi. Nandivarman Pallavamalla repulsed his enemies in the battle of Śaṁkaragrâma.

Since Pallavamalla seems to have been an usurper, it is probable that Chitramâya was no other than the heir to Paramêśvaravarman II., who had called his relative Râjasiṁha Pâṇḍya to help him.

As Kôchchaḍaiyan lived at the end of the VII century, his son Râjasiṁha lived in the first half of the VIII century at the time when Nandivarman Pallavamalla usurped the throne.

Let us now examine the Vêḷvikuḍi plates; from the Tamil portion, we learn that the son of Kôchchaḍaiyan gained a victory at Maṉṉikuṟichchi (perhaps Maṇṇaikuḍi) over the Pallavas; and the Saṅskṛit portion says that Râjasiṁha « defeated in battle King Pallavamalla ». Here, there is no room for any doubt, as the name of the king is stated clearly.

Again, the "bigger" plates of Śiṉṉamaṉûr say that Mâravarman Arikêsarin Parâṅkusa subdued the Pallavas at Saṁkaramaṅgai, a village which has been identified by V. Venkayya with Śaṁkaragrâma.

These events took place in the first half of the VIII century. It is also natural to identify Jaṭila Parântaka, son of Arikêsarin Parânkuśa Râjasiṁha, with Mâṟañjaḍaiyaṉ Parântaka of the inscriptions (Nos. 453 and 454 of 1906) found in the Âṉaimalai cave which give 769-70 as the exact date of this king.

This identification is justified by the fact that the poet who composed the Âṉaimalai verses was called Mâṟangari, alias, Madhurakavi Mûvêndamaṅgalappêraraiyan, exactly as the « Âjñapti » who composed the Vêḷvikuḍi record. Both of them lived at Karavandapura: We may therefore conclude with V. Venkayya that these two personages are but one and the same.

Jaṭila - Parantâka according to the Vêḷvikuḍi plates « con» quered the Kâḍava in battle at Peṉnâgaḍam on the southern » bank of the Kâvêri; the Âyavêḷ and the Kuṟumbas at the battle » of Nâṭṭukkuṟumbu.»

We know that the Pallavas were also called Kâḍavas.

Jaṭila is probably the doṉor of the Madras Museum Plates, the king mentioned in the Tirupparaṉkuṉṟam and the Trivandram Museum stone inscriptions (according to M. R. Ry. T. A. Gopinatha Rao) and the donor of the smaller Śiṉṉamaṉûr plates, whose name must have been mentioned in the missing plates.

In the bigger plates of Śiṉṉamaṉûr, we find no details either about the son of Jaṭila called Râjasiṁha (who was named after his grandfather) or about his grandson Varaguṇa.

The son of Varaguṇa was Śrîmara Parachakrakolâhala. The Sanskrit portion of Śiṉṉamaṉûr plates say that he vanquished Mâyâ-Pâṇḍya, the Kêraḷa, the king of Śiṁhala, the Pallava and the Vallabha. The Tamil portion says that he was victorious at Kuṇṇûr, at Śingaḷam, at Viḷiñam and that he repulsed the Gaṅgas, the Pallavas, the Chôḷas, the Kâliṅgas, the Mâgadhas who attacked him at Kuḍamûkku.

V. Venkayya has written: « At any rate the mention of a » Pâṇḍya prince as an enemy of the reigning king implies the » existence of conflicting interests in the family.» We have also remarked that the Singhalese are mentioned among the enemies of Śrîmâra. The king of Ceylon joining Mâyâ-Pâṇḍya enables us to make an identification:

In chapter LI of Mahâwaṁsa (Translation of Wijesinha) it is said (No. 27): « Now, it came to pass that at that very time a » prince of the royal family of Paṇḍu was come hither, having » formed a design to overthrow that kingdom because he had been » ill-treated by his king.»

Sena II., king of Ceylon, allied himself with the rebel Pâṇḍya prince and began to lay siege to the town of Madura.

The king of Pâṇḍyas (No. 38) « fled from the field of battle on » the back of an elephant, and gave up his life in the wrong place, » and his queen also died with him at the same time.»

According to Mahâwaṁsa, the king Sena II reigned from 866 to 901.

Here, we have to speak again about the chronology of Mahâwaṁsa.

The Chôḷas had to wage wars frequently with the kings of Ceylon and invaded that country several times.

And we know the exact dates of two of these invasions:

1° Parantaka I. invaded Ceylon a little before the 37th year of his reign (Tiruppalâturai inscr.), about 943.

2° Râjarâja conquered the island about 1002.

These invasions are of course mentioned in the Mahâwaṁsa, the first under the reign of Udaya III. and the second under the reign of Mahinda V.

But to make the dates given in the Mahâwaṁsa agree with

the correct ones, we must reduce the numbers of the Singhalese chronology by 24 years.

Besides, when we spoke of the invasion of Ceylon by Narasiṁhavarman I., we saw that the dates coincided, when we took away a little more than a quarter of a century from those given in the Mahâwaṁsa.

Subject to this condition, we may safely depend upon the Mahâwaṁsa chronology and admit that Sena II. reigned from 841 to 876 and that the Pâṇḍya king who was dethroned by his relative was probably Śrîmâra Parachakrakolâhala.

We must here note a new coincidence. The Sinnamanûr plates say that Śrîmâra encountered the Pallavas in the battle of Kuḍamûkku.

There is no doubt that in the time of the ancient Pâṇḍyas, in the IX century, the town of Kumbhakôṇam was called Kuḍamûkku; in the inscription of Mâṛañjaḍaiyan-Pâṇḍya (No. 13 of 1908) in the Nâgêsvara temple at Kumbhakôṇam, this town is called Tirukkuḍamûkku.

And we have also learnt from the Bâhûr plates, that, in the first eight years of his reign, *i.e.*, from 854 to 863, if our chronology be correct, Nṛipatuṅga gained a victory over the Pâṇḍyas on the banks of the river Arichit which M. R. Ry. T. A. Gopinatha Rao has identified with Ariśilâṛu that runs near Kumbhakôṇam.

We have said that Śrîmâra was a contemporary of Sena II who reigned from 841 to 876 and that the first eight years of Nṛipatuṅga's reign fall between 854 and 863.

We may therefore suppose that the Pallava Nṛipatuṅga profited by the invasion of the Pâṇḍya kingdom by the Singhalese, to march against Śrîmâra who was defeated at Kumbhakôṇam. The alliance of Nṛipatuṅga and Sena II. seems to be confirmed by the Bâhûr plates which say that Nṛipatuṅga's fame had spread beyond the seas as that of Râma.

The Singhalese chronicles say that the Pâṇḍya king was slain. It was perhaps about 860.

In the foregoing pages we have tried to show the importance of a knowledge of Pâṇḍya history for the proper understanding of that of the Pallavas.

The Pallava Dynasty.

- The father of "Yuvamahârâja" Śivaskandavarman (cir. A. D. 200) (King of Kâñchî) — Mayidavôlu.
- Hirahadagalli. — Śivaskandavarman (King of Kâñchî)
- Vijaya-Skandavarman (King of Kâñchî) — Guṇṭûr district.
- Chendalûr.
  - Skandavarman
  - Kumâravishṇu (I)
  - Buddhavarman
  - Kumâravishṇu (II) (King of Kâñchî)
- Vishṇugôpa (cir. A.D. 338) (king of Kâñchî) Allâhâbâd Pillar insc.
  - Kumâravishṇu (cir. A.D. 366)
  - Skandavarman (cir. A.D. 394)
  - Vîravarman (cir. A.D. 422)
    - Siṁhavarman (cir. A.D. 478)
      - Skandavarman (cir. A.D. 506)
      - Nandivarman I. (cir. A.D. 534) (king of Kâñchî)
    - Yuvamahârâja Vishṇugôpa (cir. A.D. 478)
      - Siṁhavarman (cir. A.D. 506)
      - Vishṇugôpavarman (cir. A.D. 534) (king of Palakkada)
      - Siṁhavarman (cir. A.D. 562).
        - Siṁhavishṇu (cir. A.D. 590)
          - Mahêndravarman I. (cir. A.D. 618)
          - Narasiṁhavarman I. (cir. A.D. 646)
          - Mahêndravarman II. (cir. A.D. 660)
          - Paramêśvaravarman I. (cir. A.D. 674)
          - Narasiṁhavarman II. (cir. A.D. 700)
          - Paramêśvaravarman II. (cir. A.D. 715)
        - Bhîmavarman
          - Buddhavarman
          - Âdityavarman
          - Gôvindavarman
          - Hiraṇyavarman
          - Nandivarman II. (cir. A.D. 742)
          - Dantivarman (cir. A.D. 800)
          - Nandivarman III (cir. A.D. 840)
          - Nṛipatuṅga (cir. A.D. 875)

Aparâjita (end of the IX century).

CHAPTER VI.

ESSAY ON THE HISTORY OF THE DYNASTY OF NANDIVARMAN.

§ 1. Nandivarman Pallavamalla (about A. D. 717-779).

When Paramêśvaravarman II. died, the succession was probably disputed. There was perhaps an heir belonging to the dynasty of Siṁhavishṇu who is called "Chitramâya" in the Udayêndiram plates. There was, however, at this time, a Pallava prince, called Hiraṇyavarman who claimed to be a descendant of a brother of Siṁhavishṇu and had great power in the kingdom. He was supported by some nobles: one of his friends was the "Muttaraiyaṉ", a vassal of the Pallavas, who governed the principality of Tanjore which served as a buffer state between the Pallava and the Pâṇḍya territories (*vide*: Some insc. of the Muttaraiyars by T. A. Gopinatha Rao—Journal of the S. I. Association—July 1911.)

Another friend of Hiraṇyavarman was Udayachandra who governed Vilvala (probably Villivalam) on the banks of the Vêgavatî, not far from Kâñchîpuram. (Udayêndiram plates).

Hiraṇyavarman succeeded in having his own son Nandi, then a minor, crowned at Kâñchî. (*G.O.*, No. 492, 2nd July 1906, p. 61).

Chitramâya, however, managed to obtain the help of many kings among whom were Râjasiṁha (Têr Mâraṉ), king of the Pâṇḍyas who was related to him, and perhaps also the king of the Maḷavas (father-in-law of Râjasiṁha) and the king of the Western Gaṅgas, a relation of Râjasiṁha Pâṇḍya.

The Pâṇḍyas were overthrown at Śankaramangai and Maṇṇaikudi (Maṇṇikuṟichchi) which is probably Maṇṇi near Tiruvisalur and Iḍavai (not far from Kumbhakôṇam).

The other enemies were beaten back in all directions up to the confines of the Eastern Châlukyan kingdom in which Vishṇurâja (Vishṇuvardhana III) was reigning (A.D. 709 to 746).

About 741, Vikramâditya II. (733 to 746) led the fourth Châlukyan invasion to "Tuṇḍâka" (Toṇḍai-Maṇḍalam).

In the Kêndûr plates (*Ep. Ind.* Vol. IX, No. 29, p. 205), the Châlukyas say that Vikramâditya II. « beat and put to flight, at » the opening of the campaign, the opposing *Pallava* king named » *Nandipôtavarman*, took possession of particular musical instru- » ments, called *Katumukhavâditra* and *Samudraghôsha*, the *Khat-* » *vânga-dhvaja*, many excellent and well-known intoxicated ele- » phants and a heap of rubies, which dispelled darkness by the » brilliancy of the multitude of their rays, who entered, without » destroying it, the city of *Kâñchî*, which was, as it were, a girdle » adorning yonder lady, the region of the south, who had rejoiced » Brâhmanas and poor and helpless people by his uninterrupted » liberality, who acquired high merit by restoring heaps of gold to » the stone temples of *Râjasimhêsvara* and other gods, which had » been caused to be built by *Narasimhapôtavarman*, who distressed » *Pâṇḍya*, *Chôla*, *Kêrala*, *Kalabhra* and other kings.»

The last phrase seems to show that the Pâṇḍyas joined the Pallavas.

The donations made to the Kailâsanatha temple at Kâñchîpuram by Vikramâditya II. are confirmed by an inscription caused to be cut in this temple by this king (*Ep. Ind.* Vol. III., No. 48, p. 359.)

That Nandivarman Pallavamalla reigned for a long time is confirmed by five documents :

47th year : inscription No. 55 of 1887 at Viriñjipuram.
50th year : „ No. 10 of 1895 at Pañchapâṇḍavamalai.
52nd year : „ No. 27 of 1887 at Śadupperi.
58th year : Tâṇḍanttôttam copper plates.
62nd year : inscription No. 76 of 1889 at Tiruvallam.

The last inscription mentions that the Bâna king Mavali Vanarayar was a vassal of the Pallavas.

§ 2. Dantivarman (about A. D. 779-830).

The Vêlûrpâḷaiyam plates (*S.I.I.*, Vol. II, Part V, p. 511) tell us that Nandivarman Pallavamalla had for wife Rêvâ, « who, like » (the river) Rêvâ, had (her) birth from a great king (or, from a » high mountain) » ; and it was of her that Dantivarman was born. The name Danti seems to be of Râshtrakûta origin ; and Rêvâ was probably the daughter of a Râshtrakûta king named Danti.

This will explain the political relations that subsisted at this period between the Pallavas and the Râshṭrakûṭas.

In 780—probably at the beginning of the reign of Dantivarman—the king of Kâñchî helped Gôvinda II. in his struggle against Dhruva. The latter succeeded however in dethroning his brother. (*Ep. Ind.* Vol. III., No. 17 p. 104).

There is no doubt that at this epoch the Pallava kings reigned not only in Kâñchî, but also over the region on the banks of the Kâvêrî up to the modern Pudukôtta State. In fact, in the 5th year of his reign, donations have been made at Kunnândârkoīl (Pudukotta) (No. 348 of 1914) and at Tiruvellarai (near Trichinopoly) (No. 541 of 1905).

Inscriptions were engraved in the 6th year at Tondur, near Gingee (No. 283 of 1916), and in the 7th (No. 80 of 1898), 9th (No. 74 of 1898) and 10th years (No. 51 of 1898) of his reign at Uttaramallur (Chingleput district.)

The inscriptions at Triplicane (Madras) [No. 234 of 1903—*Ep. Ind.* Vol. VIII., No. 29, p. 291], and at Kûram (No. 35 of 1900) near Kâñchî are dated in the 12th year of his reign.

In the 16th year, Dantivarman was still reigning in the Muttaraiyar kingdom, for we see that Viḍêlviḍugu Muttaraiyan̠ declared himself a vassal in two of the Malaiyaḍipatti inscriptions (Nos. III and IV, p. 23—Some inscriptions of the Muttaraiyars—Journal of S. I. Association—July 1911.)

Inscription No. 61 of 1892 at Uttaramallûr is dated in the 21st year of his reign, *i.e.*, in 800 according to our chronology.

It is about this time that Govinda III, « having conquered Dantiga, who ruled over Kâñchî,» forced Dantivarman to pay him tribute (*Ind. Ant.* Vol. XI., p. 127).

It is probable that this event considerably weakened the power of the Pallavas. It is, in fact, very remarkable that there is no inscription dated between the 21st and the 49th years of the reign of Danti 800-828.

We have two inscriptions dated at the end of Danti's reign. In the 49th year of his reign, a grant was made to Gudimallam (No. 226 of 1903) when the Bâna king Vijayâditya was the vassal of the Pallavas; and the Tiruchchân̠ûr inscription is dated in the 51st year (No. 262 of 1904).

It is remarkable that no inscription dated at the end of Danti's reign has been found in the southern portion of the

Pallava empire and particularly in the Tanjore and the Trichinopoly districts.

The name of Danti is not mentioned in any of the monuments found on the banks of the Kâvêrî, for a period of 35 years, *i.e.*, from the 16th year (Malaiyaḍipaṭṭi) to the end of his reign.

This period extends from 795 to 830 and it is strange that not a single donation was made during this time. We shall now proceed to make a remark:

A dozen inscriptions have been found:

No. 17 of 1907	No. 364 of 1907	No. 84 of 1910
No. 51 of 1895	No. 358 of 1907	No. 105 of 1905
No. 414 of 1904	No. 13 of 1908	No. 690 of 1905
No. 413 of 1904	No. 10 of 1899	

which seem to prove that the southern part of the Pallava kingdom was occupied by the Pâṇḍyas, from the 4th to the 16th year of the reign of a Pâṇḍya king called Mâṟañjadaiyan; it appears to have been a military occupation.

It is impossible to suppose that this occupation took place during the reign of the Pallava kings that succeeded Dantivarman, for, from the beginning of the reign of Nandi of Teḷḷâṟu to the advent of the Chôḷa king Parantaka, we have a series of inscriptions that will not allow us to suppose that the Pâṇḍya invasion took place at this epoch.

There are, in fact, inscriptions in the Tanjore and the Trichinopoly districts dated in the 6th (Tiruveḷḷaṟai), 10th (Tillasthânam), 12th (Śendalai), 18th (Kôvilaḍi and Tiruchchennambûṇḍi), 22nd (Tiruppalâttuṟai) years of the reign of Nandi, son of Danti; in the 7th (Nârthâmalai), 18th (Kôvilaḍi), 21st (Kaṇḍiyûr), 22nd (Lâlguḍi and Kôvilaḍi) years of the reign of Nṛipatuṅga; in the 2nd, 5th, 6th, 7th (Tiruveṟumbur) years of the Chôḷa king, Âditya.

We cannot, therefore, possibly suppose that the Pâṇḍyas occupied the banks of the Kâvêrî after the reign of Dantivarman.

So, we think that this occupation took place at the end of Danti's reign, about 825; and it is precisely this date that we have given to Varaguṇa when we studied the history of the Pâṇḍyas. It would therefore appear that king Mârañjadaiyan whose inscriptions are found on the banks of the Kâvêrî is Varaguṇa « who united Chôḷa and Toṇḍa to Madura » [Prinsep's lists made from Hâlâsya-Mahâtmyam and Tiruviḷaiyâḍal Purâṇam].

Perhaps, it was the same Varaguṇa that during the reign of Sena I., *i.e.*, from 821 to 841 (the Mahâvamsa dates being reduced by 25 years) conquered Ceylon.

Be that as it may, the inscriptions enable us to give a history of the invasion of the Pallava kingdom.

The attack began with an expedition into Iḍavai (insc. No. 690 of 1905) « in the Chôḷa country » which can be identified with the town of the same name in the Maṇṇi-nâdu (*S.I.I.* Vol II., part V, Introduction, page 23), *i.e.*, in the same nâdu as Tiruviśalûr where there is an inscription (No. 17 of 1907) of Varaguṇa-Mahârâja. And the Trichinopoly and the Ambâsamudram inscriptions tell us that Varaguṇa destroyed Vembil which is probably Tiruviśalur that was originally called Vêmbaṟṟûr.

All the Chôḷa country was conquered ; for, the inscriptions found at Tillasthânam (No. 51 of 1895) and at Trichinopoly (No. 414 of 1904) that are dated in the reign of Mâṟañjaḍaiyaṉ mention Varaguṇa.

All these inscriptions being dated in the 4th year, it is probable that the campaign was conducted at that time.

Other inscriptions :

4th + ? year at Trichinopoly (No. 413 of 1904),
6th year at Âḍuturai (No. 364 of 1907),
8th year at Âḍuturai (No. 358 of 1907),
8th year at Kumbhakôṇam (No. 13 of 1908),
10th year at Śendalai (No. 10 of 1899),
13th year at Tiruveḷḷaṟai (No. 84 of 1910),

prove that the occupation of Pallava territory was durable.

The Śendalai inscription, methinks, is specially important for fixing the date of Varaguṇa. We see that Vidêlviḍugu Muttaṟaiyaṉ lived in the 16th year of the reign of Dantivarman (Malaiyaḍippaṭṭi inscriptions) and that he made a donation at Niyaman (Śendalai) in the tenth year of Mâṟañjaḍaiyaṉ's reign.

That shows well that the invasion of Varaguṇa Pâṇḍya took place in the reign of Dantivarman.

The Ambâsamudram inscription which is dated in the 16th year of the reign of Varaguṇa Mahârâja (No 105 of 1905) is the latest in date concerning the occupation of Pallava territory. It says, that, at this period, Varaguṇa was encamped in the town of Araiśûr which is situated in the Toṇḍai-nâḍu, on the banks of the Pennar.

At this time the Pâṇḍyas had overrun half the Pallava empire and probably were preparing to march on Kâñchîpuram.

Who was the Pallava king that repulsed the invader? We shall now try to discover it.

§ 3. Nandi of Teḷḷâṟu (about 830-854).

The mother of Nandi, son of Danti, was a Kadamba princess named Aggaḷanimmaṭî. The Vêlûrpâḷaiyam plates that contain this information add that he had to fight for the throne of his father: « (V. 20). This (Nandivarman), puffed up with the » prowess of his arms, acquired the prosperity of the (Pallava) » kingdom, not easy for others to obtain, by killing (his) enemies » on the battle-field ». There is here perhaps an allusion to the battle of Teḷḷâṟu which was fought within the first ten years of his reign, since the Tillasthânam inscription (No. 52 of 1895) dated in the 10th year gives Nandi the title of Teḷḷâṟṟeṟinda.

Who was the enemy with whom he fought this battle? Very probably, it was the Pâṇḍyas. The poem Nandikkalambagam, the hero of which is Teḷḷâṟṟeṟinda, tells us, in verse 64, that he was victorious on the banks of the Vaigai (river in Madura) [*Ind. Ant.* Vol. XXXVII, page 172].

The town of Teḷḷâṟu is undoubtedly the village of Tellâr which was once the capital of Teḷḷâṟṟuppaṟṟu (insc. No. 73 of 1908) and now forms part of the Wandiwash tâluq of the North Arcot district. The existence of this town during the Pallava period has been proved in Pallava Antiquities Vol. I. page 69: I have, in fact, found in this place numerous remains of temples built in the Pallava style.

Is it rational to suppose that the Pâṇḍyas advanced as far as Tellâr which is only at a distance of 30 miles south of Kâñchipuram?

It is, on the contrary, very probable, if we admit that, at the end of Danti's reign, the southern portion of the Pallava empire was invaded by the Pâṇḍyas. We know that at the end of this occupation, Varaguṇa was encamped at Araiśur which is situated on the Pennar river in Toṇḍai-maṇḍalam (Ambâsamudram insc., No. 105 of 1905).

We may suppose, that, at the accession of Nandi, Varaguṇa tried to seize the rest of the Pallava empire and marched on Kâñchî. Nandi stopped the invader at Tellâr, inflicted many defeats on him, notably at Paḷaiyâru (Nandikkalambagam, verse 31) alias Paḷaiyârai near Kumbhakôṇam and pursued him up to the banks of the Vaigai.

This glorious campaign in which Nandi earned the surname of Teḷḷâṟṟeṟinda enabled him to reign peacefully not only at Kâñchî, (insc. No. 12 of 1895) but also on the banks of the Kâvêrî.

In the country round Tanjore and Trichinopoly, we find some inscriptions of the victor of Teḷḷâṟu, in the 10th year of his reign, at Tillasthânam (No. 52 of 1895), in the 12th year, at Śendalai (No. 11 of 1899), in the 18th year, at Kôviladi (No. 283 of 1901), and in the 22nd year, at Tiruppalâtturai (No. 180 of 1907).

The Vêlûrpâḷaiyam plates tell us that he reigned in the Nâyar region (Saidapet tâluk- Chingleput district).

More in the north, he reigned at Gudimallam where the Bâna king Vikramâditya was his vassal: (insc. No. 229 of 1903 and No. 1, *a* of 1890—*S.I.I.* Vol III., No. 42, page 93).

His reign was also rich in poets. We have already referred to Nandikkalambagam ; there were also other works :

« It was probably during the reign of this Pallava king that » the poet Perundêvaṉâr, the author of a Tamil poem entitled » Bâratavenbâ, flourished, because in the invocatory verses of the » Uttiyôgaparvam of this poem, he refers to his patron as the » Pallava king " who conquered his enemies at Teḷḷâṟu "............

« The invocatory verses prefixed to the Tamil works Puṟa- » nâṉûru, Aganâṉûru, Naṟṟiṇai, Kuṟondogai and Aiṅguṟunûṟu are » believed to have been composed by the same Perundêvaṉâr » (*G.O.* Nos. 922, 923, 19th Aug. 1899, p. 6).

§ 4. Nṛipatuṅga (about 854-880).

The Bâhûr plates give us a minute account of the birth of this king. Nandivarman (III) had married Saṅkha, a princess of the Râshtrakûta family, and their son was Nṛipatuṅga. This name having been borne by the Râshtrakûta king Amôgha-varsha I. who reigned from 815 to 879, there is little doubt that Śaṅkhâ was the daughter of Amôghavarsha I. (*Ep. Ind.*, Vol. IV., p. 181).

The Bâhûr plates tell us that Nṛipatuṅga was young when he came to the throne and that the beginning of his reign was glorious, for, he overcame the Pâṇḍyas on the banks of the Arichit.

We have already spoken about this event. M. R. Ry. T. A. Gopinatha Rao has identified this river with the Ariśil which is only another name for the Araśil (Vide *S.I.I.* Vol. II., p. 52); and the Araśil or the Araśileiyâru is but the well-known Arsalar that flows eastwards near Kumbhakôṇam and falls into the sea at Karikal.

We have already said that the adversary of Nṛipatuṅga was Mâravarman Parachakrakolahala who encountered the Pallavas at Kudamukku (Kumbhakonam), on the banks of the Arichit (Ariśil).

The Bâhûr plates compare the glory of Nṛipatuṅga to that of Râma which calls to our mind the island of Ceylon; we have already mentioned that Sena II. and Mâyâ-Pâṇḍya were allied with Nṛipatuṅga and that it was at the end of this campaign (about 861) that Madura was taken.

The Bâhûr plates belong to the 8th year of his reign, and, if our chronology is correct, their date must be about 862 shortly after the capture of Madura.

Nṛipatuṅga seems to have been a peaceful and glorious king, as a great many inscriptions dated during his reign are found scattered all over the Pallava kingdom from Tiruvâlaṅgâḍu (Nos. 460 and 461 of 1905) and Tiruvoṛṛiyûr (No. 162 of 1912) in the north, to Kaṇḍiyûr (No. 17 of 1895), Kôviladi (Nos. 303, 301 and 300 of 1901) and Lâlguḍi (No. 84 of 1892) in the south. Besides this, the Gudimallam (No. 228 of 1903) and the Nârthâmalai (No. 365 of 1904) inscriptions show that the Bâṇa king [Vidyâdhara] in the north and the Muttaraiyaṉ king [Śâttam-Paḷiyili] in the south were his vassals, so that Nṛipatuṅga's domination extended from the river Swarnamukhi in the north to the Southern Vellaur in the south, *i.e.*, from Kâḷahasti to Pudukôṭṭa.

Again, as these inscriptions are dated at the beginning as well as at the end of his reign, we have to conclude, that, during all the 26 years of his reign, the glory of Nṛipatuṅga was never eclipsed.

§ 5. Aparâjita.

We have a dozen inscriptions in which Aparâjita is mentioned; he was a Pallava king, since, in inscriptions Nos. 159 and 190 of 1912, we find the title "Pôttaraiyar" affixed to his name.

These inscriptions are dated between the 3rd and the 19th year of his reign.

They are:

3rd year	No. 351 of 1908	at	Mâṅgâḍu,
4th year	No. 158 of 1912	at	Tiruvoṟṟiyûr,
4th year	No. 161 of 1912	at	Tiruvoṟṟiyûr,
4th year	No. 31 of 1912	at	Satyavêḍu,
5th year	No. 32 of 1912	at	Satyavêḍu,
6th year	No. 190 of 1912	at	Tiruvoṟṟiyûr,
7th year	No. 163 of 1912	at	Tiruvoṟṟiyûr,
8th year	No. 159 of 1912	at	Tiruvoṟṟiyûr,
12th year	No. 180 of 1912	at	Tiruvoṟṟiyûr,
18th year	No. 435 of 1905	at	Tiruttaṇi,
18th year	No. 433 of 1905	at	Tiruttaṇi.

There is also an inscription dated in the reign of Tribhuvanavîra-dêva found at Uttaramallur which refers to the 19th year of the reign of Aparâjita.

We may add here that the village of Ukkal (near Mâmaṇḍûr) bore the name of Aparâjita-Chaturvêdimaṅgalam (*S.I.I.*, Vol. III, p. 2).

We know with certitude of two events that took place in the reign of Aparâjita:

1° *The battle of Srîpuṟambiya* (Tiruppirambiyam).

The Udayêndiram plates tell us that the Pâṇḍya king Varaguṇa fought at Srîpuṟambiya with king Aparâjita and his ally, the western Gaṅga Pṛithvîpati I. (*G. O.* No. 492, 2nd July 1906—Part II, No. 9, p. 64). The latter was slain in that battle.

As the last inscription of the reign of Pṛithvîpati I. is dated 879, it must be admitted that the battle of Śrîpuṟambiya took place after this date, *i.e.*, after 879.

Varaguṇa has been identified with a Pâṇḍya king of that name who ascended the throne in 862-63 (insc. No. 705 of 1905).

The Chôḷas were perhaps the allies of Varaguṇa, for, inscription No. 337 of 1912 seems to mention the Pâṇḍyas and the Chôḷas as the enemies of the Western Gaṅga Pṛiduvayya.

2° *The downfall of the Pallavas and the conquest of Âditya.*

The Tiruvâlaṅgâḍu plates say (Verse 49) that the Chôḷa king Âditya I. defeated the Pallava king Aparâjita in battle and took possession of his kingdom (*G. O.* No. 492, 2nd July 1906, p. 65).

Inscriptions Nos. 286 and 287 of 1911 seem to show that, in this campaign, Âditya, had as his ally the Chêra king Sthâṇu-Ravi (*G.O.* No. 919, 29th July 1912, Part II., No. 11, p. 61).

We have said above that Toṇḍai-Maṇḍalam was conquered before the 21st year of the reign of Âditya, *i.e.*, before 900. A.D. (*G.O.* No. 503, 27th July 1907—Part II., No. 29, page 71).

It is therefore incontestable that Aparâjita lived at the end of the IX century and that he was the last king of the Pallava dynasty.

There is another interesting question: What place does Aparâjita hold in the Pallava genealogy?

There are two theories concerning this subject:

1° V. Venkayya (*G.O.* No. 492, 2nd July 1906, Part II., No. 9, page 64) has supposed that Aparâjita was the son of Nṛipatuṅga.

In that case we must admit that Nṛipatuṅga was killed in the battle of Śrîpurambiya and that his son who was present at the battle succeeded to the throne and assumed at the same time the title of Aparâjita (the unconquered.)

The provinces of Tanjore and Trichinopoly would have remained in the possession of the Chôḷa prince, who, at the battle of Śrîpurambiya, was crowned king of Chôḷas under the name of Âditya I.

But Toṇḍai-Maṇḍalam continued to belong to Aparâjita who reigned there for about 20 years from 880 to 900 A.D., and it was only in the 20th year of his reign and that of Âditya that the latter succeeded in taking it with the help of the Chêras.

In support of this theory, we may point out that the inscriptions of Aparâjita are found only in the northern parts of the Tamil country, at Mangâḍu, Tiruvoṟṟiyûr, Satyavêdu, Tiruttaṇi, Uttaramallur, and none are known to exist in the Tanjore and Trichinopoly regions.

On the contrary, we know from inscriptions No. 222 of 1911 (2nd year—at Tirunâgêśvaram) and Nos. 101, 104, 105, 127, 130, 133 of 1914 (5th, 6th and 7th years—at Tiruveṟumbur) that Âditya I. held sway on the banks of the Kâvêrî in A.D. 882, 885, 886, 887. On the other hand, « It is not possible to explain why Tiru- » voṟṟiyûr, in which so many Gaṅga-Pallava epigraphs have been » discovered, should not contain any record belonging to the reign » of Râjakêsarivarman (Aditya I). Perhaps, the northern corner of » Toṇḍai-Maṇḍalam in which Tiruvoṟṟiyûr is situated had not yet » been completely brought under subjection by him.................... » (*G.O.* No. 961, 2nd Aug. 1913. Part II. No. 18, p. 94).»

It must, however, be noted that the Tiruvoṟṟiyûr temple contains 6 inscriptions dated in the 4th, 6th, 7th, 8th, and 12th years of the reign of Aparâjita while there is none belonging to Âditya.

2° M. R. Ry. T. A. Gopinatha Rao (the Pallavas and the Gaṅga-Pallavas— Madras Christian College Magazine— April 1907) has put forth the theory that the name Aparâjita was but a pseudonym of Nṛipatuṅga.

In favour of this, we may say that in case Aparâjita was no other than Nṛipatuṅga there would have been only one battle, that of Śrîpurambiya.

If, on the contrary, Aparâjita is supposed to be the son of Nṛipatuṅga, there must have been two conflicts: 1° the battle of Śrîpurambiya about the year 880 where Aparâjita would have defeated the Pâṇḍya king Varaguṇa; 2° the conquest of Toṇḍai by Âditya about the year 899 in which Aparâjita would have been himself defeated.

It is to be hoped that new discoveries would be made that might go to confirm one or other of these two hypotheses.

CONCLUSION.

In the preceding pages, we have tried to increase our knowledge of the history of the Pallavas.

No doubt, there are still many points that are obscure, many details that must be stated with precision, but I am convinced that the main facts are, after all, known to us.

1° *The Pallavas before Simhavishnu.*

A large number of copper plates (Mayidavôlu, Chendalûr, Ômgôḍu, Udayêndiram, Chûra, etc.) have proved the ancientness of the Pallava family; but these records mention isolated dynasties which it was difficult to connect with one another; and the relationship existing between these kings and the dynasty of Siṁhavishṇu was completely ignored. The Vâyalûr inscription has given us the key to most of these mysteries.

We have assumed that the first Pallava who became king owed his position to his marrying the daughter of the Andhrâ king towards the end of the 2nd century of the Christian Era.

The Vâyalûr inscription seems to indicate that kings Skandavarman - Kumâravishṇu - Buddhâvarman, whose names have been revealed to us by the Chendalûr plates, must have reigned before Vishṇugôpa, the adversary of Samudragupta, about 339 A.D.

The Udayêndiram plates give us the genealogy: Skanda—Siṁha—Skanda—Nandi; but these plates have been looked upon with suspicion. It was not known if they were a copy of an authentic record or a forgery committed by an impostor.

The Vâyalûr inscription that has given us an absolutely identical pedigree has proved the authenticity of the Udayêndiram genealogy.

Besides, the discovery, in the Vâyalûr inscription, of the series, Vîra-Skanda-Siṁha, which is identical with Uruvupalli genealogy, proves that Siṁhavarman who reigned at the time of the Uruvupalli grant was but the grandfather of Nandi of the Udayêndiram plates.

Lastly, the Vâyalûr inscription, in which we find the series Siṁhavarman - Vishṇugôpa - Siṁhavarman - Siṁhavishṇu, is the first record that gives a correct list of the names of the immediate predecessors of Siṁhavishṇu.

The deciphering of the Vâyalûr inscription has given us results which are of capital importance for the history of the predecessors of Siṁhavishṇu.

2° *The dynasty of Simhavishnu.*

The important discovery made in the State of Travancore of the work called « Mattavilâsa prahasana », and the reference to this comedy in the Mâmaṇḍûr inscription have thrown much light on this portion of history.

There is no longer any room to doubt that it was Mahéndravarman I., son of Siṁhavishṇu, that cut the caves of Mâmaṇḍûr, Vallam, Dalavânûr, Śîyamangalam, Mahêndravâdi, Pallâvaram, Trichinopoly.

So, we now possess very precise information about the saintly king Mahêndravarman I., poet, musician, architect and administrator, who introduced in South India the art that obtained on the banks of the Kṛishṇâ and gave a new impulse to religion and literature in the Tamil country.

In « Pallava Antiquities » Vol. I, I have asserted, that, to determine the age of the sculptured rocks of Mahâbalipuram, it is absolutely necessary to study the whole of the Pallava art.

In making this study, I have shown that the style of the « rathas » and caves of Mahâbalipuram belongs to the stage of transition from the style of Mahêndra to that of Râjasiṁha; there remained however a doubt: Was the Mahêndra of Trichinopoly and Pallâvaram the same as Mahêndravarman I., son of Siṁhavishṇu?

Now that all doubts on this point have been cleared, we can definitively attribute to Narasiṁhavarman I. most of the sculptures in the rock at Mahâbalipuram.

These works that were continued during the reign of Paramêśvaravarman I., were probably suspended at the time of the Châlukyan invasion which took place in 674, when Vikramâditya I., was encamped at Uragapuram (Trichinopoly).

3° *The dynasty of Nandivarman.*

There was no history of the Pallavas for the VIII and the IX centuries. The one name "Koṅkaṇika" found in the Bâhûr

plates had led the historians completely astray. M. R. Ry. T. A. Gopinatha Rao was the only one that understood the question clearly: he had affirmed that the Gaṅga-Pallava theory was quite wrong.

The defenders of that theory, however, could still argue that the name Koṅkaṇika found among the names of the ancestors of Nṛipatuṅga seemed to prove that he was not a descendant of Nandivarman Pallavamalla but of the princes of the Western Gaṅga family.

Tho deciphering of the Vâyalûr inscription has completely elucidated the question.

This inscription, which is dated in the VII century and during the reign of a king belonging to the dynasty of Siṁhavishṇu, mentions Vimala, Koṅkaṇika among the ancestors of the Pallavas.

So, the Vâyalûr inscription has removed all doubts and the genealogy of the last Pallava kings now stands established in a definite manner.

20th June, 1917. G. JOUVEAU-DUBREUIL.